Contents

Welcome to the wonderful world of vegetables. To make this book, we explored every corner of the vegie realm to provide you with an indispensable vegetable reference book. Based on years of experience developing food in the Test Kitchen and cooking for our own families at home, this is a wealth of information – you'll never have soggy roast potatoes or tasteless brussels sprouts again.

Pamela Clark
Food Director

Beautiful Vegetables

So often the silent deputy in a meal, vegetables are rarely given the chance to shine in their own right. Sometimes vegetables aren't tasty simply because they are cooked incorrectly, but with a few tricks of the trade, you can make them a family favourite. This gorgeous book helps you understand all there is to know about vegetables, including the best way to select, store and cook them.

Vegie Stars

BUYING, STORING & COOKING VEGETABLES

THE AUSTRALIAN
Women's Weekly

We've included suggested flavour pairings, and cooking instructions for every vegetable (see page 112 for information about microwaving). On page 112, you'll find a clear explanation of culinary terms and instructions on basic cooking techniques such as braising and sweating so you can prepare vegetables perfectly. This book is a celebration of beautiful vegetables, cooked well.

Artichokes

The majestic-looking globe artichoke is the large flower bud of the thistle. It is dull-green, bronze or purple. The inside of the stem tastes very similar to the heart, but needs to be peeled. Edible leaves, or petals, cover the prized heart, which is cloistered at the centre of the bud, and in the centre of the heart is the inedible furry choke. Artichokes have long been recognised as a natural digestive. Another reputed health benefit of artichokes is their cholesterol-lowering quality.

CHOOSE artichokes that have tightly packed leaves, or petals, and feel heavy for their size, with a firm stem. The leaves of small artichokes can be slightly looser, but they should still feel firm. When you pull back the leaves, the freshness should make itself known with a definite 'snap'.

STORE Artichokes start to deteriorate once picked from the thistle, so eat them as soon as possible after buying. Store them in the crisper of your refrigerator for up to 2 days.

PREPARE
Artichoke Heart Cut the stem to about 2cm to 3cm; cut 2cm to 3cm off the top of the artichoke, then snap off the leaves until you get to the heart. Scoop the furry choke out of the centre of the heart with a teaspoon. Place the prepared artichoke hearts in acidulated water as you go to prevent them browning, then boil, steam or microwave.

Whole Artichokes Remove a couple of the tough outer leaves, then cut the stems so the artichoke sits flat. For leaves and heart only, leave whole; for stuffed artichoke, cut 2cm to 3cm off the top, then scoop out the choke before cooking. When cooking several artichokes, make sure they are of similar size to ensure even cooking.

Artichoke leaves are most commonly eaten in France and Italy, but are overlooked in many other cuisines. The leaves are pulled off a whole boiled artichoke one by one, and dipped in herbed butter, then scraped against the teeth to extract the soft flesh at the base of each leaf.

RAW artichoke hearts can be sliced and tossed in a salad.

BOIL Place artichoke hearts in a large saucepan of boiling water; boil, uncovered, for about 30 minutes or until tender when pierced. Boil whole artichokes upright in a large saucepan of water for about 40 minutes or until leaves can be easily pulled out. Use a plate to weigh them down while boiling so they remain submerged.

STEAM artichoke hearts for about 40 minutes; steam whole artichokes for about 50 minutes or until leaves can be easily pulled out.

MICROWAVE Artichoke hearts are suitable to cook in a microwave oven.

PAN-FRY cooked artichoke hearts in a little butter until brown and crisp.

ROAST cooked artichoke hearts in a buttered shallow flameproof dish, briefly, until crisp.

MARINATE cooked artichoke hearts in olive oil, garlic and herbs; they are delicious on homemade pizza, especially with sliced marinated chicken breast.

STUFF cooked whole artichokes by placing the stuffing between leaves and into the cavity left by the choke. Roast for a short time to develop a little crispness.

Prepare artichoke hearts by snapping off the tough outer leaves and peeling the stem.

Cut 2cm to 3cm off the top of the artichoke heart to reveal the choke within.

Cut the heart in half from top to bottom, then scoop out the furry choke in the centre.

Artichokes with lemon herb butter

80g butter, softened

2 teaspoons finely grated
lemon rind

1 tablespoon finely chopped
fresh flat-leaf parsley

2 teaspoons finely
chopped fresh basil

4 medium globe artichokes
(800g)

1 Combine butter, rind and herbs in small bowl. Place on piece of plastic wrap; shape into log, wrap tightly. Freeze until firm.

2 Meanwhile, remove and discard tough outer leaves from artichokes. Trim stems so that artichoke bases sit flat.

3 Cook artichokes in large saucepan of boiling water about 40 minutes or until tender; drain.

4 Serve hot artichokes topped with slices of herb butter, and lemon wedges.

prep & cook time 50 minutes (+ freezing) **serves** 4
nutritional count per serving 16.7g total fat
(10.8g saturated fat); 723kJ (173 cal);
1.9g carbohydrate; 3.9g protein; 1.2g fibre

Asian greens

Asian vegetables have become very accessible and are now available in supermarkets. They support strong salty flavours as well as garlic, chilli and nut-based oils. These greens are a great accompaniment to chicken and firm white fish.

CHOOSE greens that look fresh and crisp, not dry. To ensure they're fresh, accept only a touch of yellow on a couple of the outer leaves.

STORE in the refrigerator for 2 to 3 days only.

VARIETIES

1. Buk choy (bok choy) and baby buk choy

Buk choy is usually bought in bunches of 3 or 4 plants. It has a crisp, fresh taste – quite similar to cabbage with an acidic tang. Wash thoroughly in water to rid the leaves of hiding bugs. Both stems and leaves are edible. Cook baby buk choy stems and leaves together; larger, older buk choy stems need a slightly longer cooking time than the leaves.

BLANCH buk choy in plenty of boiling water, uncovered, for about 2 minutes.

STEAM buk choy for about 3 minutes.

MICROWAVE Buk choy is suitable to cook in a microwave oven; stir midway through cooking time.

STIR-FRY For baby buk choy, halve or quarter, or for larger buk choy separate whole leaf and stem from base of plant, then stir-fry for about 30 seconds or until limp.

Drain well before drizzling buk choy with a warm Asian-style sauce.

2. Choy sum and baby choy sum

Otherwise known as flowering buk choy or flowering cabbage, this Asian vegetable is closely related to buk choy. It has much longer, more slender stems and leaves and small yellow flowers, all of which are edible and can be cooked together. It has a similar taste to buk choy with a mild mustard flavour.

BLANCH choy sum in plenty of boiling water, uncovered, for about 4 minutes.

STEAM choy sum for about 4 minutes or until limp and deep green.

MICROWAVE Choy sum is suitable to cook in a microwave oven; stir midway through cooking time.

STIR-FRY Add whole pieces of choy sum to the wok and stir-fry for about 30 seconds or until limp.

Drain well before drizzling with a salty or chilli sauce.

The wide leaves of the larger plant can be used as a parcel package – blanch briefly, then wrap around fish and pan-fry.

3. Gai lan

Gai lan is the delicious steamed green vegetable eaten in yum-cha restaurants. It is also known as chinese broccoli because of its flavour, although, unlike broccoli, the most prized part of the gai lan is its stem. Though not often used, the leaves and small white flowers are also edible.

PREPARE gai lan by cutting away most of the large leaves from the stems, leaving just a few centimetres of the leaves attached to the stem.

BLANCH gai lan stems in plenty of boiling water, uncovered, for about 3 minutes or until deep green but still slightly crisp. Drain well.

STEAM gai lan stems for about 4 minutes or until tender.

MICROWAVE Gai lan is suitable to cook in a microwave oven; stir midway through cooking time.

STIR-FRY gai lan stems for about 30 seconds or until limp.

Make a traditional dressing by combining warmed sesame oil and oyster sauce; pour over hot blanched gai lan.

4. Tatsoi

Also called rosette buk choy, tatsoi is a slightly tougher version of buk choy. It has the same taste as buk choy, but its leaves are darker and more glossy; its larger leaves are tougher and require longer cooking. Smaller, more tender leaves are eaten raw in salads. Tatsoi has a very short shelf life.

PREPARE Separate leaves from root system, then wash briefly to remove any soil.

RAW This is the most common way to eat tatsoi. Use the smaller, more tender leaves in salads with more conventional greens, or as a side dish to white fish.

BLANCH tatsoi in plenty of boiling water, uncovered, for about 3 minutes.

STEAM larger leaves for about 5 minutes or until tender.

MICROWAVE Tatsoi is suitable to cook in a microwave oven; stir midway through cooking time.

STIR-FRY smaller leaves for about 30 seconds or until limp.

ADD smaller leaves to soups at the end of the cooking time.

Stir-fried choy sum

1 tablespoon peanut oil
1 fresh long red chilli,
   sliced thinly
2 cloves garlic, crushed
2cm piece fresh ginger
   (10g), grated
1kg choy sum, trimmed,
   cut into 5cm lengths
2 tablespoons fish sauce
2 tablespoons lime juice
1 cup (150g) roasted
   unsalted cashews

1 Heat oil in wok; stir-fry chilli, garlic and ginger 1 minute.
2 Add choy sum; stir-fry until almost tender. Add sauce and juice; stir-fry until hot.
3 Serve stir-fry sprinkled with nuts.
prep & cook time 15 minutes **serves** 4
nutritional count per serving 23.6g total fat
(4.1g saturated fat); 1271kJ (304 cal);
10g carbohydrate; 10.4g protein; 6.1g fibre

Baby buk choy salmon parcels

2 teaspoons peanut oil

10cm stick fresh lemon grass
(20g), chopped finely

1 fresh kaffir lime leaf,
chopped finely

1 fresh small red thai chilli,
chopped finely

1 clove garlic, crushed

2cm piece fresh ginger
(10g), grated

600g skinless salmon fillets,
cut into 1cm pieces

6 baby buk choy (900g)

2 tablespoons kecap manis

1 Heat oil in small frying pan; cook lemon grass, lime leaf, chilli, garlic and ginger, stirring, 2 minutes or until fragrant. Cool.

2 Combine salmon and lemon grass mixture in medium bowl.

3 Press salmon mixture into centre of each buk choy; wrap leaves around filling, tie with kitchen string to secure.

4 Place buk choy parcels in large bamboo steamer over large saucepan of boiling water; steam, covered, about 10 minutes or until salmon is cooked as desired.

5 Cut parcels in half; serve drizzled with kecap manis.

prep & cook time 40 minutes **serves** 6

nutritional count per serving 8.9g total fat
(1.9g saturated fat); 744kJ (178 cal);
1.8g carbohydrate; 21.6g protein; 2.1g fibre

1.   2.   3.

Asparagus

VARIETIES

1. Green asparagus varies from very thick to very thin stems. When they are in season (spring to summer) asparagus typifies the taste of spring; crunchy and deliciously fresh-tasting.

2. Purple asparagus was originally an Italian cultivar. It is sweeter than green and white asparagus and can be eaten raw in salads. When cooked, it takes on a mildly nutty flavour. With brief cooking, it will retain its purple colour, although with longer cooking it will turn the familiar green hue.

3. White asparagus is made by denying the growing plant chlorophyll-producing sunlight. Dirt is mounded up around the stem as it grows, stopping the sunlight from reaching it. White asparagus tastes slightly more bitter, is more fibrous or stringy and toughens faster than the green variety, although it has a more delicate aroma.

Because of its fresh, clean and slightly woody taste, asparagus is at its most glorious when its own flavours are allowed to be the star of the show. It is highly regarded and used in Asian cooking, particularly in Thailand, and also in Chinese cooking where it is dressed simply in a thin sauce that allows the flavour of the vegetable to shine through.

In French cooking, it is mostly accompanied by a perfectly poached egg or a creamy sauce such as hollandaise. In Italy, it is often paired with salty flavours such as anchovy or prosciutto.

CHOOSE asparagus with stalks that do not look dry, split or withered at their cut end. The stems should not be moist, but clean and dark green. As soon as asparagus is harvested it begins to lose flavour and juiciness, and becomes more fibrous from the bottom up. So freshness is of paramount importance.

STORE asparagus upright in the fridge for up to 2 days with their cut ends in water and plastic wrap draped over the tips and secured to the container with a rubber band.

PREPARE by snapping off the woody bottoms. Gently bend the asparagus at the base and it will snap at its natural breaking point – where the woodiness turns into crispness. Traditionally, the tough skin at the bottom 3cm of the asparagus is peeled with a vegetable peeler, although this is becoming less necessary as varieties develop. White asparagus, needs peeling from the bottom right up to the tips.

STEAM, BOIL or MICROWAVE
If asparagus ends are much thicker than the tips, cut them into pieces and cook them first then add the tips a minute or so later. Cook for the shortest possible time to achieve the best texture and colour. Remove asparagus from the heat while still bright green. Cooked asparagus should not flop when held upright. Arrest the cooking process by very briefly plunging it into cold water. Adding citrus juice or vinegar to cooked asparagus can wrinkle and discolour the skin.

BOIL Add to boiling water; boil, uncovered, for 3 minutes.

STEAM asparagus for about 4 minutes. It can be steamed in a special asparagus steamer (see page 114).

MICROWAVE Asparagus is suitable for cooking in the microwave oven.

STIR-FRY asparagus for 3 to 5 minutes.

GRILL or BARBECUE for an intense flavour. Steam larger stems for 2 minutes, then grill 1 minute on each side. Coat young, tender asparagus with cooking-oil spray then grill or barbecue without pre-steaming.

Hold uncooked asparagus close to the base of the spear. Bend until it snaps; discard the woody end.

Asparagus with poached egg and hollandaise

1 tablespoon white wine
   vinegar
2 egg yolks
200g unsalted butter,
   melted
500g asparagus, trimmed
2 tablespoons white vinegar
4 eggs
¼ cup (20g) shaved
   parmesan cheese
1 tablespoon coarsely
   chopped fresh dill

1 Blend or process white wine vinegar and egg yolks until smooth. With motor operating, gradually add butter in a thin, steady stream, processing until hollandaise thickens.
2 Meanwhile, boil, steam or microwave asparagus until tender; drain.
3 Add white vinegar to medium deep frying pan of gently simmering water. Break one egg into a cup, then slide into pan; repeat with remaining eggs. Cook eggs, uncovered, about 2 minutes or until white is set and yolk is still runny. Remove with slotted spoon; drain on absorbent paper.
4 Serve asparagus topped with eggs, hollandaise, cheese and dill.
prep & cook time 35 minutes **serves** 4
nutritional count per serving 51.4g total fat
(30.9g saturated fat); 2153kJ (515 cal);
1.7g carbohydrate; 12.6g protein; 1.3g fibre

Avocados

VARIETIES

1. Hass

The most popular avocado variety is the hass. It has a lusciously creamy, nutty, almost sweet-tasting flesh and very little stringy fibre. A large round seed is enclosed tightly in its cavity. Its peak season is early summer. At other times of the year, small woody buds are sometimes attached to the inside of the skin. It is the only variety that changes colour (a deep purple) when ripe.

2. Shepard

The shepard is a small, green-skinned, pear-shaped avocado that does not change colour upon ripening. It has a fairly mild flavour, sometimes rubbery flesh, a large seed and peels easily. They are more resistant to blackening once cut than other varieties as long as the seed is replaced in the remaining avocado and it is covered tightly with plastic wrap. Shepard avocados are at their best in autumn.

The buttery richness of a perfectly ripe avocado is one of the great offerings from the vegetable world. Its Mexican and American heritage encourage us to eat avocado with anything corn-based, such as corn chips, tortillas, and corn fritters – especially in the form of that perennial favourite: guacamole. Avocado is a particularly good partner for white fish or shellfish, and added chilli or fresh herbs such as parsley, mint or coriander, gives it a lively taste. Anything citrus, especially lemon and lime, adds a zippy dimension to the smooth texture of the avocado flesh.

They are not usually cooked, but when heated, avocados change flavour dramatically and get a slightly 'eggy' flavour. Most simply it is mashed on toast, sliced into a salad, diced as part of a salsa or just drizzled with a simple vinaigrette and eaten with a spoon.

CHOOSE Buy avocados several days in advance, when they are quite hard, and let them ripen in your fruit bowl at home. This is best for transporting them, too, as they tend to bruise very easily when ripe. A ripe avocado should have only a small amount of give when you cradle it in the palm of your hand and squeeze the neck very gently.

STORE avocados at room temperature for the best quality texture and flavour. You can accelerate ripening by storing them next to ripe bananas (or, even better, store avocados and ripe bananas in a paper bag together). Only store in the refrigerator once ripe.

PREPARE The simplest method for getting the stone out of the avocado doesn't involve stabbing at the seed with a knife. Cut the avocado lengthways, moving around the stone; twist to separate the two halves. Keep the seed in the half of the avocado it is left in until you need that half. Cradle it in the palm of your hand with the widest end away from you. Using the fingertips of your other hand, pry the seed up and out starting from the wide end.

To peel, you can either scoop the flesh out carefully with a large spoon, or simply peel the skin back from the flesh and chop or slice as required. Once cut, keep the surface from becoming brown by sprinkling it with a citrus juice, such as lime or lemon, or by covering it completely and removing all oxygen from the wrapping making it airtight. If you have made guacamole in advance for a party, keep it from turning brown by pressing plastic wrap directly onto the surface.

Tomato-stuffed avocado halves

2 large avocados (640g)
2 large tomatoes (440g), seeded, chopped finely
1 small red onion (100g), chopped finely
2 tablespoons olive oil
2 tablespoons lime juice
2 tablespoons finely chopped fresh coriander
¼ teaspoon Tabasco sauce

1 Halve avocados; remove and discard seeds. Using a large spoon, carefully remove avocado flesh from skin in one piece; discard skin.
2 Combine remaining ingredients in small bowl.
3 Serve avocado halves topped with tomato mixture.
prep time 20 minutes **serves** 4
nutritional count per serving 34.5g total fat (6.8g saturated fat); 1442kJ (345 cal); 4.1g carbohydrate; 3.7g protein; 3.4g fibre

Beans

VARIETIES

1. French baby green beans have slightly smoother, darker green skins than mature green beans. They are crunchy and crisp with a very grassy flavour.

2. Green beans are sweeter and juicier than the baby variety, though have a slightly tougher texture.

3. Snake beans are very long, malleable beans; they can be tied into knots for cooking and are often used in stir-fries. They are sweet with an almost mushroom-like flavour.

4. Yellow beans are just like green beans – without the chlorophyll. As a result they taste less 'green' and are slightly less flavoursome than green-coloured beans.

5. Flat beans have a tough texture and a grassy flavour with a slightly earthy taste.

6. Roman beans, or continental beans, are very sweet and juicy, although their appearance is rather dry with a satin finish to the skin. Slice and use in salads or keep whole as a side dish.

7. Borlotti Beautiful, spring-time borlotti beans have a speckled pink and cream skin, as do the beans inside. They need to be shelled: carefully unzip the pod along the seam and let the beans fall out. Add cooked borlotti beans to a fresh, homemade tomato sauce for a ham-like, nutty flavour. Mix with silver beet instead of bacon for a tasty vegetarian option, or use in an Italian soup.

8. Broad beans, or fava beans, usually need to be 'double-peeled' (*see Prepare, right*). Their flavour is musky and fresh, and they combine beautifully with mint and fetta in a salad, or slip easily into a spring vegetable soup. Early in the season they are sweet; later in the season, when they become mealy, they should be pureed.

Beans are part of the legume family – famous for their protein (and infamous for their propensity to cause flatulence). Beans are most often served warm as a side dish to a meat, fish or poultry main course or as a starter, simply stacked on a plate with a basic dressing as simple as some garlicky herbed melted butter or an easy vinaigrette. Try warm beans topped with toasted nuts or breadcrumbs. Beans are also lovely with just a little burnt butter.

CHOOSE fresh beans that are immature and small as they start to lose their sugar content once picked. Choose those that feel crisp to the touch. Broad beans should be moist-looking and green, yellow, snake and roman beans should be crisp and bright.

STORE beans in the refrigerator for up to 2 days. Broad beans can be frozen in a freezer bag once podded.

PREPARE green, roman, flat, yellow and snake beans by cutting up to 1cm off their tops and tails. Longer beans can be cut into required lengths.
To double-peel broad beans, first remove the beans from the foamy inside of the pod, then blanch the beans for about 1 minute in boiling water; run under cold water until cool enough to handle then slip the layer of springy grey skin from the bean. You will be left with a tender green bean. Cook for 1 minute longer to serve them as is, or continue with your recipe.

COOK beans until almost tender though retaining a little crunch. Do not over-cook or the nutrients will be leached into the boiling water and the beans will be limp and grey. When boiling, use plenty of rapidly boiling, lightly salted water. Rinsing under cold tap water after cooking helps to arrest the dulling of the colour.

BOIL Add beans to boiling water; boil baby green, green, snake, yellow, flat and roman beans, uncovered, for about 5 minutes. Boil broad beans, for about 2 minutes and borlotti beans for about 20 minutes.

STEAM baby green, green, snake, yellow, flat, roman and broad beans for 5 minutes or until just tender. Steam borlotti beans for 30 minutes.

MICROWAVE Beans are suitable for cooking in the microwave oven. Borlotti beans take longer than other varieties.

STIR-FRY beans for about 3 to 5 minutes. Snake beans are especially good for stir-frying.

Broad bean and ricotta orecchiette

375g orecchiette pasta

1 tablespoon olive oil

2 cups (300g) fresh shelled broad beans

1 clove garlic, crushed

½ cup (125ml) cream

1 teaspoon finely grated lemon rind

2 tablespoons lemon juice

200g ricotta cheese, crumbled

½ cup coarsely chopped fresh mint

1 Cook pasta in large saucepan of boiling water until tender; drain.

2 Meanwhile, heat oil in large frying pan; cook beans and garlic until beans are just tender. Add cream, rind and juice; simmer, uncovered, until sauce thickens slightly.

3 Combine pasta, sauce and remaining ingredients in large bowl.

prep & cook time 30 minutes **serves** 4

nutritional count per serving 25.2g total fat (13.4g saturated fat); 2500kJ (598 cal); 67.4g carbohydrate; 21.3g protein; 7.9g fibre

Prosciutto-wrapped bean bundles

200g green beans, trimmed
200g yellow beans, trimmed
8 slices prosciutto (90g)
60g butter
1 tablespoon rinsed, drained
  baby capers
1 tablespoon lemon juice
⅓ cup coarsely chopped
  fresh flat-leaf parsley

1 Cook beans in medium saucepan of boiling water until just tender. Rinse under cold water; drain. Divide beans into eight equal bundles.
2 Place one slice of prosciutto on board; top with one bundle of beans. Wrap prosciutto over beans; continue rolling to enclose beans tightly. Repeat with remaining prosciutto and beans.
3 Cook bean bundles in heated oiled large frying pan until prosciutto is crisp. Remove from pan; cover to keep warm.
4 Melt butter in same pan; cook capers, stirring, 1 minute. Stir in juice.
5 Serve bean bundles drizzled with caper mixture; sprinkle with parsley.

prep & cook time 30 minutes **serves** 8
nutritional count per serving 6.9g total fat
(4.3g saturated fat); 347kJ (83 cal);
1.5g carbohydrate; 3.3g protein; 1.5g fibre

Beetroot

VARIETIES

1. Beetroot has an earthy bitterness combined with a sweetness derived from its relatively high sugar content (about 20% sucrose). The surprisingly harmonious result makes beetroot suitable for both savoury and sweet recipes. Mature varieties are usually about the size of a cricket ball. When cooked, beetroot remains firm in texture, though less crisp than when raw.

2. Baby beetroot are picked when immature, and are usually the size of a golf ball. They do not bleed as much as their mature counterpart, and can be slightly sweeter though otherwise taste the same. Baby beetroot are good to use if you want to keep them whole in your recipe.

3. Golden baby beetroot are slightly more mild in flavour. It should be prepared in exactly same way as red beetroot. The pigment in this beetroot does not stain as deeply as the red.

4. Baby beetroot leaves look very much like baby spinach leaves, with red stems and veins coursing through the dark green leaf. They are often found in a mesclun salad mix (a mixed greens salad mix). They have a peppery, earthy taste. Use just as you would baby spinach leaves.

With its gorgeous hue, beetroot can't help but be a startling inclusion in any recipe. Of course, their permeating colour can either be a feature or a distraction. Wearing disposable gloves is one way to avoid staining your hands when cooking with beetroot. Scrub your chopping board with some kitchen salt to help remove any stains. Beetroot is fantastic with Middle-Eastern spices, garlic, horseradish, fresh herbs or piquant cheese.

CHOOSE beetroot that are firm, unblemished and certainly not mouldy. Only buy beetroot that has some of the stem remaining as any cut into the bulb will cause too much bleeding during cooking.

STORE for up to 4 days in the crisper in the refrigerator.

PREPARE beetroot for boiling, roasting or eating raw by trimming stems to 2cm and scrubbing clean with a soft-bristled brush. Don't trim the beard at the base of the plant.

RAW beetroot can be grated and served with a vinaigrette or thinly sliced into a salad; add it last to prevent an overly red look. The brilliant colour and taste of beetroot is fantastic in a zesty juice with ginger and orange.

BOIL Add beetroot to a large saucepan of boiling water and boil, covered, for about 20 minutes for baby beetroot and about 45 minutes for medium-sized beetroot. Insert a thin skewer into the widest part to test for doneness; it should slide easily through. Cool for 10 minutes, then peel with a vegetable peeler or simply split and squeeze the skin with gloved hands, the skin will slip off easily. A salad is a wonderful way to showcase beetroot. Try gently combining boiled beetroot, fetta cheese and mint with a walnut dressing.

STEAM medium-sized beetroot about 50 minutes or until tender.

MICROWAVE Beetroot are suitable to be cooked in a microwave oven; peel and cut large beetroot in half.

ROASTED beetroot has a deliciously nutty, earthy flavour. Use them as a side to a roast meal, on pizza, pureed for a dip, or in tarts or quiches. For whole beetroot, roast wrapped in foil for about 45 minutes, depending on how large they are, at 180°C/160°C fan-forced. Or chop coarsely, toss in olive oil and fresh thyme leaves and roast at 200°C/180°C fan-forced for about 30 minutes or until tender.

Turkish beetroot dip

3 medium beetroot (500g), trimmed
1 teaspoon caraway seeds
1 teaspoon ground cumin
¼ teaspoon hot paprika
¾ cup (200g) yogurt
½ cup loosely packed fresh mint leaves
2 cloves garlic, crushed
1 tablespoon lemon juice

1 Cook beetroot in medium saucepan of boiling water, uncovered, about 45 minutes or until tender; drain. When cool enough to handle, peel beetroot then chop coarsely.
2 Meanwhile, dry-fry spices in a small frying pan until fragrant; cool.
3 Blend or process beetroot, spices and remaining ingredients until smooth.
serving idea This dip is delicious with toasted turkish bread.
prep & cook time 50 minutes **makes** 2 cups
nutritional count per tablespoon 0.3g total fat (0.2g saturated fat); 67kJ (16 cal); 2g carbohydrate; 0.8g protein; 0.7g fibre

Broccoli

It seems a humble vegetable to us now, but broccoli was considered exotic when first brought to Australia by Italian immigrants in the mid-20th century. Now we hardly consider it Italian at all, although one of the most wonderful traditional Italian pasta dishes is orecchiette with broccoli and breadcrumbs (see page 25 for our version of this classic recipe). The little dark green 'flowers' on the head of the broccoli and the very small stems immediately below are referred to as florets. Both flowers and stems are edible. Serve blanched, steamed or microwaved broccoli warm and topped with almonds, mixed with green beans, or dressed in olive oil warmed in a frying pan with garlic and chilli flakes.

CHOOSE broccoli with tightly packed florets. It should be deep green – almost purple – and not tinged with yellow.

STORE in the refrigerator for up to 2 days.

PREPARE broccoli by first giving it a good wash. Cut the florets from the stems and soak them in acidulated water, which will flush out any hidden bugs. Peel the thicker parts of the stem thickly with a vegetable peeler, then slice.

BLANCH broccoli, uncovered, for just 1 to 2 minutes in lots of well-salted, boiling water for a bright green, deliciously flavoured vegetable. Dressed simply with butter, salt, pepper and nutmeg, it is an absolute delight.

STEAM for about 4 minutes; overcooking broccoli does it no justice.

MICROWAVE Broccoli is suitable to be cooked in a microwave oven.

STIR-FRY Break broccoli into tiny florets and stir-fry for 3 to 5 minutes.

PUREE steamed, boiled or microwaved broccoli to make a delicious, hearty soup. Serve with a dollop of sour cream. Stems should be cooked separately for a slightly longer time than the florets. They can then be pureed to a very fine, creamy consistency and added to the soup.

Broccoli and garlic breadcrumb spaghetti

12 slices stale white bread
500g spaghetti
300g broccoli, cut into florets
⅓ cup (80ml) olive oil
50g butter
2 cloves garlic, crushed
¼ cup (20g) shaved
    parmesan cheese

1 Remove and discard crusts from bread; process bread until fine.
2 Cook pasta in large saucepan of boiling water until tender; drain.
3 Meanwhile, boil, steam or microwave broccoli until tender; drain.
4 Heat oil and butter in large frying pan; cook breadcrumbs and garlic until browned lightly and crisp.
5 Combine pasta, broccoli and breadcrumbs in a large bowl. Serve sprinkled with shaved parmesan.
prep & cook time 25 minutes **serves** 4
nutritional count per serving 34.2g total fat (11g saturated fat); 4004kJ (958 cal); 129g carbohydrate; 27.7g protein; 10.2g fibre

Broccolini

Broccolini is the product of a naturally occurring romance between broccoli and gai lan – not the result of genetic modification. The whole vegetable is edible, even the yellow flowers that sprout from the little green buds. The flavour is generally considered to be slightly sweeter than broccoli, though the stems have a slight peppery edge. Packed with vitamins C and A, folate, iron and calcium, it is a very female-friendly vegetable. It is available year-round. Broccolini looks charming on a plate, more so than the slightly bulky broccoli, and can happily support many of the flavours that broccoli suits, so it is a fine substitute as a side dish.

CHOOSE broccolini with shiny stems and dark-green buds and leaves. Avoid broccolini with slightly yellowing foliage; sprouting yellow flowers, however, are no problem.

STORE broccolini in the refrigerator, upright with the lower part of the stems in a glass of water with a plastic bag over the top. It will last a couple of days when kept like this.

PREPARE broccolini by soaking in acidulated water to flush out bugs and dirt, then trim about 1cm from the ends of the stems and remove any leaves.

BOIL Add boccolini to boiling water; boil, uncovered, for about 2 to 3 minutes.

STEAM broccolini for about 2 to 3 minutes.

MICROWAVE Broccolini is suitable to cook in a microwave oven.

Serve broccolini with salt and pepper and warmed olive oil or a curl of butter.

STIR-FRY broccolini for about 3 to 5 minutes.

SAUTÉ broccolini with a little olive oil. Add garlic, chilli and a salty element such as anchovy or prosciutto for a lovely Italian twist.

GRILL or BARBECUE This method brings out the lovely nutty flavour of broccolini. Microwave until just changed in colour, or boil or steam for about 1 minute, then finish on the grill or barbecue for a further 1 minute on each side.

Broccolini with bacon and egg

700g broccolini, trimmed

40g butter

2 rindless bacon rashers
(130g), chopped coarsely

2 thick slices ciabatta (70g),
cut into 1cm pieces

1 clove garlic, crushed

1 tablespoon rinsed
drained baby capers

1 tablespoon finely chopped
fresh flat-leaf parsley

2 soft-boiled eggs,
chopped coarsely

1 Boil, steam or microwave broccolini until tender; drain.

2 Meanwhile, melt butter in large frying pan; cook bacon until crisp. Add bread and garlic; cook, stirring, until bread is browned lightly. Add capers and parsley; stir until hot.

3 Divide broccolini among serving plates; top with bacon mixture and egg.

prep & cook time 25 minutes **serves** 4

nutritional count per serving 16.2g total fat
(7.9g saturated fat); 1154kJ (276 cal);
9.6g carbohydrate; 19.4g protein; 7.9g fibre

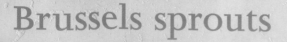

Looking just like miniature cabbages, brussels sprouts are little mouthfuls of nutritional goodness. Avoid overcooking and you will be surprised at how delicious they can be. Brussels sprouts are usually served as a side dish. The sweet cabbage flavour goes well with nuts, bacon or prosciutto, butter or herbs.

CHOOSE firm, bright green sprouts as small as you can find – the smaller the sprout, the sweeter it is.

STORE in the refrigerator for up to 2 days.

PREPARE brussels sprouts by trimming the bottoms of each sprout, and pulling away any loose discoloured leaves. Wash the sprouts well.

BOIL Add brussels sprouts to boiling water; boil, uncovered, for about 7 minutes.

STEAM for about 7 minutes, then split open and top with butter, salt and pepper for a delicious-tasting dish.

MICROWAVE Brussels sprouts are suitable to cook in a microwave oven.

SAUTÉ chopped brussels sprouts with butter and herbs until wilted. Or, remove petals individually by snapping them off at the base and pan-fry them quickly over low heat in butter and olive oil.

Brussels sprouts

Brussels sprouts with cream and almonds

50g butter

⅓ cup (25g) flaked almonds

1kg brussels sprouts,
   trimmed, halved

2 cloves garlic, crushed

300ml cream

1 Melt 10g of the butter in large frying pan; cook nuts, stirring, until browned lightly; remove from pan.

2 Melt remaining butter in same pan; cook sprouts and garlic, stirring, until sprouts are browned lightly. Add cream; bring to the boil. Reduce heat; simmer, uncovered, until sprouts are tender and sauce thickens slightly.

3 Serve sprout mixture sprinkled with nuts.

prep & cook time 10 minutes **serves** 4

nutritional count per serving 46.7g total fat (28.4g saturated fat); 2061kJ (493 cal); 6.6g carbohydrate; 9.5g protein; 7.3g fibre

Cabbages

VARIETIES

1. Green, baby green, or drumhead cabbage, is the common variety used in many cabbage recipes including sauerkraut and stuffed cabbage rolls. It has a mild, fresh taste that deteriorates with overcooking.

2. Savoy cabbage has crinkly leaves and is less tightly packed than the green or red cabbage. It tastes milder than other cabbage varieties.

3. Red cabbage is more densely packed than green or savoy, and has a slightly more bitter taste. Its striking appearance makes it a feature in coleslaw. Baby red cabbage is also available.

4. Wombok, also known as chinese cabbage, has a crunchy texture and is relatively sweet. It is the most commonly used cabbage in South-East Asia.

Cabbage goes well with pork, bacon, sausages or game. It is often paired with potato as both these vegetables are staples in many countries. Fresh, sweet apple makes a good partner for cabbage and combined they are an excellent side dish for pork. Creamy, tart dressings sit well with crunchy raw cabbage. In Asian cooking, salty sauces, ginger, garlic, chilli and green onion are common accompaniments for both raw and cooked cabbage.

CHOOSE green and red cabbage that feel heavy for their size, with frosty-looking, shiny outer leaves that look healthy and dense. If you can, buy a whole cabbage as once cut, cabbage starts to deteriorate in quality.

STORE red and green cabbage in the refrigerator for about a week. Savoy and wombok should be eaten within 2 days.

PREPARE in all cases by removing the tough outer leaves. For wombok, peel off as many leaves as required to get to those that are a lighter green. The white leaves of the green cabbage have the best flavour, so remove enough of the green leaves to reveal them. If you want to use whole boiled leaves for stuffing, do not cut the cabbage. For steaming, using in a soup or salad, pan-frying or sautéing, cut raw cabbage into quarters then cut away the core. To shred, lie flat on a cutting board and finely cut across leaves. At this point, rinse cabbage thoroughly under water and drain well, especially if using it raw. While cabbage can be boiled, it is better steamed, sautéed or pan-fried. The important rule of thumb is to ensure you do not overcook; brevity is the key.

BOIL a whole head of cabbage (for whole leaves to be used for stuffing) by immersing entirely in boiling water for 2 to 3 minutes; retrieve from the water and remove only those leaves that pry off easily. Repeat the boiling and removing of leaves until you have enough.

STEAM chopped cabbage for about 5 minutes.

MICROWAVE Chopped cabbage is suitable to be cooked in a microwave oven.

STIR-FRY cabbage for about 1 to 3 minutes or until limp.

PAN-FRY chopped or shredded cabbage in butter.

Mixed cabbage coleslaw

⅓ cup (80ml) olive oil
2 tablespoons cider vinegar
2 teaspoons dijon mustard
2 cups (160g) finely shredded green cabbage
2 cups (160g) finely shredded red cabbage
2 cups (160g) finely shredded wombok
1 medium carrot (120g), grated coarsely
4 green onions, sliced thinly

1 Whisk oil, vinegar and mustard in large bowl; mix in remaining ingredients.
prep time 20 minutes **serves** 4
nutritional count per serving 18.4g total fat (2.6g saturated fat); 836kJ (200 cal); 4.5g carbohydrate; 2.4g protein; 4.7g fibre

Capsicums

VARIETIES

1. Red capsicums are the most common. Their sweetness makes them perfect in a salad or salsa. They have very thick walls, making them stable for stuffing. They become especially sweet when cooked or char-grilled.

2. Green capsicum All capsicums start their life green, changing colour as they ripen. When green, they have a slightly tangy flavour. Once cooked, they lose their brightness, turning a dull green, and also lose some of their flavour, taking on a slight bitterness.

3. Orange and yellow capsicums are slightly less sweet than red capsicums. The combination of orange, yellow and red capsicum in a salad is visually pleasing and terrific on the tastebuds, too.

4. Baby red capsicum are about a third of the size of a mature capsicum. They have a finer skin, and are sweeter and more tender than their mature counterparts. They are excellent stuffed with mascarpone or ricotta cheese and baked.

5. Vine-sweet minicaps can be orange, red or yellow and are about the size of baby red capsicums. They are full of flavour with a crispy texture and are delicious eaten raw. They have a very fine skin and few seeds, although they still need deseeding.

6. Banana chillies Yellow, lime-green and red banana chillies are sweet and mild in flavour. They are not hot and taste much like capsicum. Like green capsicums, green banana chillies are less sweet and are better enjoyed raw.

Black capsicums (*not pictured*) are an immature capsicum, like the green variety, and have a similarly sharp taste. May sometimes be a deep purple in colour. They have thin skin and do not cook well, becoming slimy when blanched. Best used raw, and added for colour to a salad.

Though often referred to as sweet peppers, or bell peppers, capsicums don't actually belong to the pepper family at all; they are thick-walled, sweet-fleshed members of the chilli family. They do, however, mix well with hot chillies. They are essentially hollow, with a central pith studded thickly with seeds that need to be removed. The skin can be bitter and when removed, capsicums become very sweet and supple in texture. Capsicums and banana chillies go well with spanish onion, tomato, sweet corn, mushrooms, black pepper or mild, fresh cheese.

CHOOSE firm, non-wrinkled, glossy capsicums with a uniform, bright colour. They should feel heavy and the stalk should look green and fresh. Make sure you take your recipe into account when you select your capsicums and choose those with a suitable shape.

STORE uncut, unwashed capsicum in the refrigerator for up to one week.

PREPARE by first removing the seeds and the bulky internal membrane. Avoid seeds altogether and cut cheeks from the capsicum, rather than cutting through the centre pith. If you want rings of raw capsicum, or need to remove the core for stuffing, carefully cut a ring around the stalk, through the internal structure and pull out the core with a little twist. To remove the skin from the capsicum, char the skin over a naked gas flame, using a pair of tongs, until the skin is black all over. Alternatively, cut the capsicum in half, brush with a little olive oil, if you like (it works well without oil), and place in a hot oven or under a grill until blackened. Immediately after blackening, sweat the capsicums in a plastic or paper bag, or covered with plastic wrap, under an upturned bowl or between layers of absorbent paper for at least 10 minutes. The skin should then slip off easily. If not, rub the skin with a damp cloth.

RAW capsicum is lovely in a salad, on its own with a tangy vinaigrette, tossed through rice salad or in a salsa to accompany salty cheese or corn fritters.

STIR-FRY sliced or chopped capsicum for 1 to 3 minutes.

ROASTED capsicum, with seeds and skin removed, can be added to a stock and pureed for a delicious sweet soup. Or toss through pasta, or stir into rice dishes.

STUFF whole capsicum with rice, vegetable or chicken-based fillings after first removing the core and seeds. Roast in the oven until the mixture is cooked through and the capsicum is tender. Stuff baby reds or mini caps with mascarpone, cream cheese or ricotta.

MARINATE peeled capsicum in olive oil, garlic and herbs. Use marinated capsicum within 2 days tossed through pasta, on sandwiches or pizza, or in an antipasto platter.

ADD chopped raw capsicum to a casserole or curry.

Blacken the skin of the capsicum, then cover until soft and supple.

Roasted capsicum and ricotta salad

2 medium orange capsicums (400g)
2 medium red capsicums (400g)
2 medium yellow capsicums (400g)
2 medium green capsicums (400g)
80g baby rocket leaves
1 small red onion (100g), sliced thinly
1 cup (240g) ricotta cheese, crumbled
oregano vinaigrette
⅓ cup (80ml) olive oil
2 tablespoons red wine vinegar
1 clove garlic, crushed
1 tablespoon finely chopped fresh oregano

1 Preheat oven to 200°C/180°C fan-forced.
2 Quarter capsicums; discard seeds and membranes.
Place, skin-side up, on oven tray. Roast, uncovered, about
20 minutes or until skin blisters and blackens. Cover capsicum
pieces with plastic or paper for 5 minutes; peel away skin,
then slice capsicum thickly.
3 Make oregano vinaigrette.
4 Combine capsicum with rocket and onion in large bowl;
sprinkle with cheese, drizzle with vinaigrette.
oregano vinaigrette Combine ingredients in screw-top jar;
shake well.

prep & cook time 30 minutes **serves** 4
nutritional count per serving 25.6g total fat
(6.9g saturated fat); 1396kJ (334 cal);
12.4g carbohydrate; 12.3g protein; 3.9g fibre

Carrots

VARIETIES

1. Mature carrots have a distinctive aroma and a sweet, mild taste. Carrots are almost always included in stocks, stews and soups as a basis for much Italian and French cooking. Middle-Eastern flavours also pair well with carrots, particularly in a thick, fragrant soup.

2. Baby carrots are full of flavour and are wonderfully sweet. They do not need to be peeled, making them a perfect snack. Simply lop the greenery off and scrub the carrots with a clean scourer.

CHOOSE medium-sized carrots, as large ones can be a little woody. Pick those that aren't split or have too many blemishes.

PREPARE mature carrots by scraping the bitter outer layer with a knife or peeling with a vegetable peeler. Cut carrots into the required size – either julienne (matchstick-sized slices) or cut lengthways and left whole for a larger cut, or cut into thick or thin slices.

BOIL Add only enought water to cover carrots then boil, covered, for about 7 minutes.

STEAM Cut carrots into 1cm slices and steam for about 9 minutes.

MICROWAVE Carrots are suitable to be cooked in a microwave oven.

Larger pieces should be given about an extra 5 minutes to steam or boil.
Serve warm steamed, boiled or microwaved carrots with butter and tarragon or parsley.

RAW Combine coarsely grated carrot with shredded cabbage and a lemon and olive oil dressing to make a simple coleslaw. Juice with other vegetables for a great vitamin shot.

STIR-FRY Cut carrots into matchstick-sized pieces and stir-fry for 2 to 4 minutes.

PAN-FRY par-boiled carrots with a little of their boiling liquid and butter until soft and glossy.

GRILL OR BARBECUE carrot pieces for about 15 minutes for char-grilled flavour with caramelised charred stripes.

ROAST carrots for about 45 minutes at 200°C/180°C fan-forced, or until they are tender and caramelised.

PUREE boiled carrots with a pinch of roasted cumin for a delicious dip or vegetable side dish.

BAKED carrot cakes are delicious, moist and full of flavour.

PEEL long ribbons of carrot, using a vegetable peeler, to deep-fry or sauté or toss through pasta primavera.

Orange and maple-glazed baby carrots with hazelnuts

30g butter
800g baby carrots, trimmed, peeled
2 teaspoons finely grated orange rind
¼ cup (60ml) orange juice
2 tablespoons dry white wine
2 tablespoons maple syrup
½ cup (70g) coarsely chopped roasted hazelnuts

1 Melt butter in large frying pan; cook carrots, turning occasionally, until almost tender.
2 Add rind, juice, wine and syrup; bring to the boil. Reduce heat; simmer, uncovered, until liquid has almost evaporated and carrots are tender and caramelised.
3 Serve carrots sprinkled with nuts.
prep & cook time 25 minutes **serves** 4
nutritional count per serving 17.2g total fat (4.5g saturated fat); 1145kJ (274 cal); 20.8g carbohydrate; 4.1g protein; 7.7g fibre

Cauliflowers

1.

VARIETIES

1. Mature cauliflower is closely related to broccoli, and looks similar. The florets that sprout at the top of the stalks are referred to as the 'curd'. The creamy, fleshy stalk and mustardy curd gets pleasingly soft when cooked. Baby cauliflower is also available, and is a great single-serving treat; it tastes great drizzled with a white sauce.

Broccoflower (*not pictured*) is a cross between broccoli and cauliflower, producing a lime-green head. It tastes like cauliflower, although is slightly sweeter, and is prepared in the same way.

Jacaranda, or purple cauliflower, (*not pictured*) is naturally coloured with the same red properties that make red cabbage red. It is very similar in taste to the white cauliflower, with a faintly bitter, rather than overly mustard, taste. It will retain its purple colour when boiled, steamed, microwaved or roasted. A squeeze of lemon juice added to the cooking water will help keep the vibrancy of the colour intact.

Romanesco cauliflower (*not pictured*) is a bright green variety with spherical florets that closely resembles white cauliflower in taste. It does not roast well as both texture and flavour suffer. Use for a novelty effect in a stir-fry or side dish.

The creamy texture of cauliflower works well with creamy, cheesy sauces and nutmeg. It is an ideal side to white fish, as well as a Sunday roast. The subtle mustard flavours support mustard-based dressings. Cauliflower is full of folate and fibre, so it's a good nutritional source for women. When cooking cauliflower, remember that light-handed treatment is best for this vegetable. Cauliflower contains sulphur compounds similar to that of cabbage, which break down as they cook, releasing a distinctive odour that gets stronger the longer they are over heat.

CHOOSE cauliflowers that have creamy white, tightly bunched curd, without any discolouration.

STORE for a few days in the refrigerator.

PREPARE cauliflower by breaking into florets; drop into acidulated water as you go to dislodge any bugs hiding in the curd. This also improves the whiteness of the cauliflower head.

BOIL Cover cauliflower florets in lightly salted water then boil, uncovered, for about 4 minutes.

STEAM whole cauliflower (large and small) or florets for about 4 minutes, or until tender.

MICROWAVE Cauliflower is suitable to be cooked in a microwave oven; turn midway through the cooking time.

STIR-FRY small pieces of cauliflower for 3 to 5 minutes.

PAN-FRY Slice whole cauliflower into 2cm-thick slices then slowly pan-fry over gentle heat in butter for delicious results.

ROAST cauliflower in a gratin; the white and purple varieties stand up better to this preparation than romanesco.

Cauliflower gratin

6 baby cauliflowers (750g), trimmed
50g butter
¼ cup (35g) plain flour
1½ cups (375ml) hot milk
½ cup (60g) coarsely grated cheddar cheese
¼ cup (20g) finely grated parmesan cheese
1 tablespoon packaged breadcrumbs

1 Preheat oven to 220°C/200°C fan-forced.
2 Boil, steam or microwave cauliflowers until tender; drain. Place in medium shallow ovenproof dish.
3 Meanwhile, melt butter in medium saucepan, add flour; cook, stirring, until mixture bubbles and thickens. Gradually stir in milk until smooth; cook, stirring, until mixture boils and thickens. Remove from heat, stir in cheeses.
4 Pour cheese sauce over cauliflower in dish; sprinkle with breadcrumbs. Bake about 15 minutes or until browned lightly.
prep & cook time 30 minutes **serves** 6
nutritional count per serving 14.1g total fat
(9g saturated fat); 865kJ (207 cal);
10.2g carbohydrate; 9.1g protein; 2.2g fibre

Celeriac

Celeriac, sometimes called knob celery, is a member of the celery family, though it is grown as a root vegetable for its large, well-developed taproot rather than for its stems and leaves. It has white flesh with a very earthy, creamy and pungent celery-like flavour. Celeriac has quite different texture and cooking qualities from celery so it is generally not suitable as a substitute. However, it does have a similar flavour, so it is often used as flavouring in stocks, soups and stews. It goes well with parsley, creamy accompaniments, cold cut meats, and with *pinziminio*, a simple Italian dressing of olive oil, salt and pepper. Nutritionally, celeriac is low in carbohydrates.

CHOOSE celeriac that are as smooth-looking as possible, to make peeling slightly easier. They should not be soft, or too large. Don't be put off by the knobbly outer skin, as the beauty lies below the outer layer.

STORE for up to a week in the refrigerator.

PREPARE celeriac by peeling thickly with a vegetable peeler, as the outer skin is tough, warty-looking and inedible. As the white flesh is exposed to air, it becomes brown, so drop celeriac pieces into acidulated water as you go.

RAW celeriac is excellent finely cut into a salad, or coarsely grated or cut into julienne strips then mixed into a mustard-mayonnaise dressing and served with cold meat such as prosciutto or sopressa salami.

BOIL Add coarsely chopped celeriac to boiling water; boil, covered, for about 30 minutes.

STEAM coarsely chopped celeriac for about 40 minutes or until tender.

MICROWAVE Celeriac is suitable to be cooked in a microwave oven; stir midway through cooking time.

PAN-FRY cooked celeriac in butter and serve as a side.

DEEP-FRY celeriac strips for an interesting variation on chips.

ROAST celeriac, just like pumpkin, for about 1 hour at 200°C/180°C fan-forced until it is a lovely golden colour.

SAUTÉ boiled and dried pieces of celeriac for about 10 minutes.

PUREE cooked celeriac and mix with mashed potato for a delicious side dish.

ADD celeriac to a casserole.

Celeriac puree

2 cups (500ml)
  chicken stock
1kg celeriac, trimmed,
  peeled, chopped coarsely
½ cup (125ml) cream
1 tablespoon finely chopped
  fresh chives

1 Bring stock to the boil in medium saucepan; add celeriac, return to the boil. Reduce heat; simmer, covered, about 30 minutes or until celeriac is tender. Drain.
2 Blend or process celeriac in batches with cream until smooth.
3 Serve sprinkled with chives.

prep & cook time 35 minutes **serves** 4
nutritional count per serving 14.4g total fat (9.2g saturated fat); 815kJ (195 cal); 7.4g carbohydrate; 5.2g protein; 8.8g fibre

Celery

Celery is one of the basic ingredients in many cuisines; it is a crucial inclusion in stocks and sauces. It goes well with walnuts, white fish or mustard as well as creamy dressings such as a blue cheese dressing. It is closely related to fennel, so they combine well in a salad. Egg and salty ingredients, such as anchovies, olives or capers, also mix well with celery. It is available all year, with peak season being late summer to early autumn.

CHOOSE celery with fresh-looking leaves – not wilted.

STORE unwashed, in the refrigerator, wrapped in aluminium foil, for up to a week. Revive limp celery by cutting 2cm off both ends and submerging in a bowl of iced water for 30 minutes.

PREPARE celery by chopping about 10cm off the base. Trim the leaves and small stalks at the point where there is a natural 'crease' in the stem. The leaves can later be used in a stock or in a salad. To remove the 'stringy' outer layer of the celery that tends to get stuck in the teeth, simply peel the outside of the celery thinly with a vegetable peeler. In French cooking, celery, carrot and onion are all finely chopped in equal quantity to make a mirepoix (pronounced *meer pwah*), which, either raw, roasted or sautéed, is the basis for a wide number of dishes including stocks, soups, stews and sauces.

RAW celery has a crisp, fresh taste that makes it a great snack that kids love with a scoop of just about anything in its deep groove; try peanut butter or cream cheese.

STIR–FRY celery for about 1 to 3 minutes.

BRAISED celery becomes translucent, soft and smooth in flavour.

ADD peeled, chopped celery to vegetable stock and cook until tender to make a distinctively-flavoured summer soup.

Waldorf salad

¾ cup (225g) mayonnaise
¼ cup (60ml) lemon juice
5 stalks celery (750g), trimmed, sliced thickly
2 medium red apples (300g), sliced thinly
1 small red onion (100g), sliced thinly
1 cup (100g) roasted walnuts
1 cup loosely packed fresh flat-leaf parsley leaves

1 Combine mayonnaise and juice in large bowl; mix in remaining ingredients.
prep time 20 minutes **serves** 4
nutritional count per serving 35.7g total fat (3.1g saturated fat); 1852kJ (443 cal); 22.4g carbohydrate; 5.8g protein; 6.3g fibre

Corn

VARIETIES

1. Sweetcorn is juicy and creamy sweet. It is usually a pale yellow colour when raw, although polkadot varieties are available with a sprinkling of dark or light coloured kernels throughout the yellow.

2. Polkadot corn, also known as salt & pepper corn, is just another variety of sweetcorn.

3. Baby corn are immature, unpollinated ears of corn picked from full-size corn varieties. They are picked early when the cob itself is still edible and sweet. They are not sweeter than sweetcorn, and they are certainly less juicy. Baby corn is available in shops already trimmed and ready to use.

Traditional sweetcorn starts converting its sugars to starch three days after it is harvested, although modern varieties keep slightly longer with the husk on. In either case, the sooner you eat the corn, the better.

We eat sweetcorn in a huge variety of ways. Corn on the cob, ground to polenta, as cornflour, in salsas, fritters, breads, soups and, of course, as simple boiled corn with a dab of butter, a sprinkling of sea salt and a grind of black pepper.

CHOOSE corn with the husk on, removing it only at the last possible moment. The husk should be pale green, with a yellow tinge. The 'silk' or beard, that sprouts from the top should be silky (hence it's name), rather than dry.

STORE in the refrigerator with the husk on, for up to 2 days.

Corn bread

3 trimmed corn cobs (750g)
¾ cup (180ml) buttermilk
2 eggs, beaten lightly
50g butter, melted
1 cup (150g) self-raising flour
1 cup (170g) cornmeal
½ teaspoon salt
½ cup (60g) coarsely grated cheddar cheese
¼ cup finely chopped fresh flat-leaf parsley

1 Preheat oven to 200°C/180°C fan-forced. Grease deep 22cm-round cake pan; line base and side with baking paper.
2 Remove kernels from corn. Process two-thirds of the kernels with 2 tablespoons of the buttermilk until smooth. Stir in remaining kernels, remaining buttermilk, eggs and butter.
3 Sift flour into medium bowl; stir in cornmeal, salt, cheese and parsley. Add corn mixture; mix until combined. Spread mixture into pan; bake about 50 minutes. Stand 10 minutes; turn, top-side up, onto wire rack to cool.
prep & cook time 1 hour **serves** 12
nutritional count per serving 7.3g total fat (3.9g saturated fat); 874kJ (209 cal); 27g carbohydrate; 7.4g protein; 3g fibre

PREPARE Remove the husk (unless you intend to cook on a barbecue or grill plate) by stripping it back from the top down, bringing as much of the silk as possible with it. Remove kernels by making a deep cut halfway down the cob with a large sharp knife, then snapping it in two to create a stable surface at one end. Stand corn on cut edge and, taking hold of the top, carefully slide the knife down the cob behind the kernels. Continue around the cob.

BOIL Add sweetcorn cobs to boiling unsalted water; boil, covered, about 10 minutes. To test for tenderness, slip a sharp knife into a kernel.

STEAM sweetcorn cobs for about 10 minutes.

MICROWAVE Sweetcorn cobs are suitable to be cooked in a microwave oven; turn midway through cooking time.

Baby corn should be steamed, boiled or microwaved briefly; it goes well with Asian food.

STIR–FRY baby corn for 2 to 4 minutes.

BARBECUE or GRILL sweetcorn cobs with the husk on. Peel back the husk, keeping it attached at the base of the stalk; remove the silk, then put the husk back in place. Soak the cobs in water for about 3 hours or overnight to prevent scorching; cook on a hot grill for about 15 minutes, testing for tenderness at 10 minutes. Turn midway through cooking time.

Cut and snap corn in two. Use the cut sides as a stable base and run a knife down the cob to remove corn kernels.

Cucumbers

Cucumber is at its best when eaten raw, although there are recipes for cooking cucumber. Cucumber suits both tart and creamy recipes. Dill, chilli, vinegar, yogurt, fetta cheese, cream cheese, sour cream, hummus, garlic, smoked salmon or white fish all go well with cucumber.

VARIETIES

All cucumbers have a high water content with a crisp texture and fresh flavour.

1. Lebanese cucumbers have relatively thin, tender skin and smaller seeds than telegraph, green or white cucumbers. They do not require peeling; it is a matter of preference if you do or not. They are crisp and juicy and a deliciously refreshing snack.

2. Telegraph, or continental cucumbers have a thicker skin and require peeling before using in a dip, salad or soup. There is a good flesh to seed ratio, so they are less moist than other varieties.

3. Green cucumbers have a thick skin and large seeds. The seeds can be slightly bitter so are often removed from green cucumbers.

4. White, or apple cucumbers are juicy and fleshy with a sweet flavour. They have a pale skin and large seeds. Depending on how you are using the cucumber, removing the large seeds is preferable.

5. Qukes are essentially baby lebanese cucumbers. They require no preparation as they have almost no seeds and a tender skin. They are excellent as a snack.

CHOOSE glossy, firm cucumbers that have no soft spots.

STORE them in the crisper of the refrigerator for up to 3 days.

PREPARE To seed cucumbers, cut them in half lengthways, then use a teaspoon to run the length of the cucumber, scraping toward you with the spoon facing down. Peeling is a matter of preference, although the thicker-skinned varieties, such as telegraph and green cucumbers, should certainly be considered.

SLICE thinly or use a vegetable peeler to make ribbons to add to a salad, or make a salad of dill, white vinegar and cucumber. Cucumber sandwiches have a lovely aristocratic resonance that makes you feel special when eating them. Simply butter good, white bread, add thinly sliced cucumber and trim the crusts.

JULIENNE cucumber for a crudité platter with a selection of dips.

PICKLED cucumber is a classic accompaniment for cold meats or as a pre-dinner snack.

CHOP a seeded cucumber finely then mix with yogurt, garlic and lemon for tzatziki, a traditional Greek dip.

Thai cucumber pickle

6 lebanese cucumbers
   (780g), halved
      lengthways, seeded
¼ cup (60g) coarse
   cooking salt
2 cups (500ml) rice vinegar
½ cup (110g) caster sugar
2 tablespoons fish sauce
2cm piece fresh ginger
   (10g), grated
2 cloves garlic, crushed
1 fresh long red chilli,
   sliced thinly
1 small red onion (100g),
   sliced thinly

1 Place cucumber in colander; sprinkle with salt. Stand 2 hours. Rinse well under cold water; drain. Pat dry with absorbent paper. Slice cucumber into 1cm-thick slices.
2 Combine vinegar, sugar and sauce in medium saucepan; stir over heat until sugar dissolves. Add ginger, garlic and chilli; bring to the boil. Remove from heat.
3 Place cucumber and onion in sterilised jars; pour vinegar mixture over cucumber. Seal jars tightly; cool. Refrigerate overnight.
cook & prep time 30 minutes (+ standing & refrigeration)
makes 4 cups
nutritional count per ¼ cup 0.1g total fat (0g saturated fat); 205kJ (49 cal); 10.8g carbohydrate; 0.7g protein; 0.8g fibre
tip Pickle can be stored, in the refrigerator, for up to two weeks.

4.

4.

3.

Eggplants

VARIETIES

1. Regular eggplant is the most common variety used in Western cooking. Use this variety when a lot of flesh is required, for example, in baba ghanoush (a smoky eggplant dip).

2. Baby eggplant goes by many names: lebanese, finger, japanese and long tom. These long, slender eggplants do not need to be disgorged (sprinkled with salt to draw out the bitter juices). Their texture differs slightly to that of their larger counterparts being slightly less 'furry' on the palate, otherwise, they taste and can be used in the same way.

3. Thai pea eggplants are slightly larger than a green pea and of similar shape and colour; they are sold fresh, in clusters like grapes, or pickled in jars. They are more bitter than the larger thai apple eggplant, with which they can be substituted in many Thai recipes. The bitterness is a necessary foil to the richness of sweet coconut-based curries. They are seasonal, and can be bought in Asian grocery stores and some greengrocers.

4. Thai apple eggplants are hard and of golf ball size; they are usually pale green traced with white in colour, but can also be purple with a white blush, or a creamy white colour. They look like small unripe tomatoes and are very popular in both Thai and Vietnamese cooking. They are crisp and tart in flavour with lots of bitter seeds that should be removed before using.

Regular and baby eggplant are used in many cuisines – Italian eggplant parmigiana, Arabic Imam bayaldi, Greek moussaka, French ratatouille and, of course, baba ghanoush from the Middle East. They are also very popular in Asian and Indian cooking. Thai and pea eggplants add flavour and a tart punch to Thai curries. Pair eggplant with sesame seeds or oil, salty cheese, chilli, tomato, sweet sultanas, asian and mediterranean herbs and creamy or cheesy sauces.

CHOOSE shiny, firm, heavy eggplants without discoloured soft spots.

STORE in a cool, dark, dry place for up to 2 days. Keep cold storage to a minimum as chilling damage will turn them brown and bitter.

PREPARE The requirement to disgorge the eggplant of its bitter juices is becoming irrelevant as newer, less bitter varieties are developed. Disgorging involves sprinkling salt over cut surfaces of the eggplant and leaving on a rack for 30 minutes to draw out bitter juices. In particular, baby, thai and pea eggplants do not need to be disgorged. Use a vegetable peeler to peel strips, in intervals, off a whole eggplant before slicing into rounds; this will increase its tenderness when cooked.

STIR-FRY sliced regular or baby eggplant for about 5 to 7 minutes.

PAN-FRIED Raw eggplant is a sponge for oil, soaking it up and leaving little for the pan, thus making the cooked product very rich. Precook eggplant (grill or barbecue) prior to frying in oil to minimise this absorption.

BARBECUE or GRILL thinly sliced pieces of regular or baby eggplant on a lightly oiled barbecue or grill plate on both sides until tender and browned. Serve on an antipasto platter or marinate in olive oil and use later on a sandwich or homemade pizza.

ROAST whole regular or baby eggplant, pierced all over, in an oiled shallow flamproof dish for 1 hour at 200°C/180°C fan-forced.

PUREE the flesh of a roasted or smoked eggplant for a dip.

SMOKE over a direct flame (such as the flame of a gas stovetop) for an authentic Middle-Eastern flavour.

SIMMER all eggplant varieties in a sauce or curry.

Eggplant parmigiana

2 large eggplants (1kg)
vegetable oil, for shallow-frying
½ cup (75g) plain flour
4 eggs, beaten lightly
2 cups (200g) packaged breadcrumbs
750ml bottled tomato pasta sauce
1 cup (100g) coarsely grated mozzarella cheese
¼ cup (20g) finely grated parmesan cheese
⅓ cup loosely packed fresh oregano leaves

1 Using vegetable peeler, peel random strips of skin from eggplants; discard skins. Slice eggplants thinly.
2 Heat oil in large frying pan.
3 Coat eggplant in flour; shake off excess. Dip in egg, then in breadcrumbs. Shallow-fry eggplant, in batches, until browned lightly. Drain on absorbent paper.
4 Preheat oven to 200°C/180°C fan-forced.
5 Spread about one-third of the pasta sauce over base of greased 2.5-litre (10-cup) ovenproof dish. Top with about one-third of the eggplant, one-third of the cheeses and one-third of the oregano. Repeat layering.
6 Bake, covered, 20 minutes. Uncover; bake about 10 minutes or until browned lightly.
prep & cook time 1 hour **serves** 6
nutritional count per serving 27.7g total fat (6.6g saturated fat); 2266kJ (542 cal); 49.4g carbohydrate; 19.9g protein; 8.3g fibre

Fennel

Fennel has a strong aniseed flavour and onion-like texture. It is a large bulbous vegetable, about 8cm to 12cm in diameter, with a large swollen base consisting of several overlapping broad stems, forming a white to very pale green-white, firm, crisp bulb. The stems come to a stalk at the top, like celery, and sprouts feathery fronds (leaves). All these parts can be used: the fronds are used as a herb to flavour fish or potato salad, but can also be used to add a subtle aniseed flavour to pasta and rice dishes. The stalk can replace celery in stock or soup for a different depth of flavour. The bulb can be eaten raw or cooked in any number of ways. Fennel can be paired with poultry, white fish, orange, olives, salty hard cheese or fresh-tasting vegetables such as celery.

VARIETIES

1. Fennel is common to many cuisines around the world. It is used as a digestive in Italy, eaten raw at the end of a meal. In India, fennel seeds are provided in homes and restaurants to chew after eating. The aniseed flavour is very strong when fennel is raw, but cooking brings out its natural sweetness.

2. Baby fennel is simply a small fennel and can be used as a substitute for mature fennel. Because of its smaller size, it is more suitable for recipes that require whole or halved fennel. It is also available all year round whereas larger fennel is best as a spring vegetable.

CHOOSE fennel using a smell test: a sweet, not sour, smell indicates freshness. Look for upright green fronds and a bulb that's not bruised or slimy.

STORE for up to 3 days in a plastic bag in the refrigerator. Fennel loses its flavour quickly, so use as soon as possible.

PREPARE Remove the outer layer of the bulb as it can be tough. Trim a very thin slice from the base then cut the bulb in half from top to bottom. Use a small sharp knife to gouge the pyramid-shaped core out of the base. Slice fennel as required.

RAW fennel goes well with spring onion, peppery salad leaves, orange, lemon juice or parmesan. Slice very thinly.

BLANCH trimmed and halved fennel in boiling water for about 5 minutes or until tender.

STEAM trimmed and halved fennel for about 5 minutes or until tender.

MICROWAVE Fennel is suitable to be cooked in a microwave oven.

STIR-FRY for 2 to 4 minutes.

GRILL thick slices slowly for wonderfully sweet results.

ROAST thick pieces until soft and caramelised. Drizzle with a little balsamic vinegar near the end of the cooking time.

BRAISE in white wine or other cooking liquid. Fennel will absorb the flavour of the braising liquid.

Caramelised fennel tarts

50g butter
4 baby fennel bulbs (520g), trimmed, halved lengthways
1 teaspoon finely grated orange rind
½ cup (125ml) orange juice
1 sheet ready-rolled puff pastry
2 teaspoons finely chopped fresh thyme

1 Preheat oven to 220°C/200°C fan-forced. Grease and line two oven trays.
2 Melt butter in large frying pan; cook fennel until browned lightly. Add rind and juice; bring to the boil. Reduce heat; simmer, uncovered, about 5 minutes or until fennel is caramelised and tender.
3 Cut pastry sheet into four squares; place on oven trays. Remove fennel from pan, leaving behind the pan juices; divide among pastry squares. Bake about 20 minutes or until pastry is browned.
4 Meanwhile, return pan juices to the boil. Reduce heat; simmer, uncovered, until sauce thickens slightly.
5 Serve tarts drizzled with sauce and sprinkled with thyme.
prep & cook time 45 minutes **serves** 4
nutritional count per serving 19.8g total fat (11.9 saturated fat); 1145kJ (274 cal); 19.9g carbohydrate; 3.3g protein; 2.7g fibre

Jerusalem artichokes

Jerusalem artichokes have a knobbly, uneven surface, but under the skin, their creamy colour and consistency is worth the peeling effort. They have a delicious and distinctively nutty taste, like hazelnuts or chestnuts, and a crisp and crunchy texture, like a water chestnut. They are of the same family as yam or potato, and can be treated in a similar way. They are available all year round, but are cheaper and better during the cooler months. Jerusalem artichoke is the tuber of a species of sunflower, so it is also known as a sunchoke. The Italian word for sunflower is girasole which, over time, morphed into an English-sounding version of the word: jerusalem. It is thought the artichoke part of the name comes from its early introduction to Europe from North America where it was described as tasting similar to the globe artichoke.

CHOOSE hard jerusalem artichokes with the smoothest surface possible to make peeling an easier job. Avoid those that are sprouting.

STORE in a cool, dark, dry place. They will last for at least a week.

PREPARE by scrubbing first, then peeling with a vegetable peeler, starting with the knobbly sections to create as smooth a surface as possible before peeling the rest of the vegetable. The white flesh browns upon contact with oxygen so drop into acidulated water as you peel them.

Although they taste great, jerusalem artichokes have been known to cause severe flatulence. This effect can be alleviated by adding 1 teaspoon of asafetida to the cooking water for each 500g of vegetable. This powdered spice, often used in Indian cooking, has a very strong sulfur (rotten egg) smell, though this diminishes with cooking. Asafetida is available in speciality food stores or delicatessens with the dried herbs and spices.

RAW Slice very thinly, with a mandolin or V-slicer and toss into a salad with a lemon-based dressing.

BOIL Cover with water then boil, covered, for about 30 minutes or until tender.

STEAM for about 20 minutes, or until tender, then mash with cream or butter for a creamy, nutty-flavoured mash.

ROAST with a little olive oil, salt and pepper, as you would for potato.

SAUTÉ boiled then dried pieces of jerusalem artichoke for about 10 minutes.

PUREE jerusalem artichoke that has been boiled in a vegetable stock for a delicious, creamy soup.

Jerusalem artichoke crisps

1kg jerusalem artichokes, unpeeled, sliced thinly
2 tablespoons olive oil
1 teaspoon salt
½ teaspoon cracked black pepper

1 Preheat oven to 200°C/180°C fan-forced.
2 Combine ingredients in medium bowl; place artichoke slices, in single layer, on wire rack over large baking dish. Roast about 20 minutes or until crisp.
prep & cook time 30 minutes **serves** 4
nutritional count per serving 9.4g total fat (1.3g saturated fat); 619kJ (148 cal); 7.6g carbohydrate; 5.3g protein; 6.8g fibre

Leeks

Leeks are part of the onion and garlic family, and can perform a similar pivotal role in innumerable recipes. Like onion, leeks soften and reduce in volume as they caramelise, creating a subtle, sweet flavour. Leeks have a particular kinship with chicken and the two are often paired. A sharp counterpoint such as anchovy, capers or mustard balances the sweetness of leeks beautifully.

VARIETIES

1. Mature leeks have a mild onion flavour and are slightly cabbage-like and creamy in texture. They make an ideal substitute for onion, and give a more subtle, delicate edge to a dish.

2. Baby pencil leeks are simply immature leeks. They are often cooked whole, as a starter or side dish.

CHOOSE leeks with as much white as possible, as that is the section to use in cooking. Look out for, and avoid, leeks with yellowed leaves or those that look dry and discoloured. The green parts are tougher than the white, and have a more cabbage-like taste.

STORE for up to a week in the crisper of the refrigerator.

PREPARE leeks by removing two outer layers, cut off the green tops and trim off the roots, keeping ends intact. To remove any trapped dirt, split leeks in half lengthways, fan out and rinse under the tap. Sliced leeks can be rinsed in a colander under the tap. For baby leeks, cut a slit 2cm deep into the top of each leek and rinse.

2.

1.

BOIL Tie baby leeks in bundles of three, place in a saucepan; cover with cold water then bring to the boil. Simmer, covered, for about 10 minutes or until tender. Serve with a simple vinaigrette.

BRAISE sliced mature leeks with some white wine and vegetable stock.

STIR-FRY leeks for about 5 minutes; they should retain a slightly crunchy texture.

PAN-FRY leeks until they have caramelised; use in a tart or quiche. Add chicken to form the basis of a chicken and leek pie.

DEEP-FRIED or crispy leeks are a delicious finger food.

SWEAT leeks and add potato and vegetable stock, then puree for French vichyssoise – cold leek and potato soup.

SUBSTITUTE leek for onion in pies, stocks, stews and creamy sauces or cook slowly with butter in any recipe that has an onion base.

Halve leeks lengthways, then fan out and rinse under the tap.

Braised baby leeks

16 baby pencil leeks
  (1.3kg)
30g butter
⅔ cup (160ml) chicken stock
2 tablespoons dry white wine
1 teaspoon finely grated
  lemon rind
2 tablespoons lemon juice
¼ cup (20g) flaked
  parmesan cheese
¼ cup coarsely chopped
  fresh flat-leaf parsley

1 Carefully trim root end from leeks, leaving each leek in one piece. Trim leeks into 15cm lengths; halve lengthways. Rinse under cold water; drain.

2 Melt butter in large frying pan; cook leek, 1 minute. Add stock, wine, rind and juice; bring to the boil. Reduce heat; simmer, covered, 15 minutes or until leek is tender. Uncover; simmer about 5 minutes or until liquid has reduced by half.

3 Serve leek drizzled with cooking liquid then sprinkled with cheese and parsley.

prep & cook time 40 minutes **serves** 4
nutritional count per serving 8.7g total fat
(5.2g saturated fat); 644kJ (154 cal);
8.3g carbohydrate; 6.5g protein; 6g fibre

Mushrooms

WILD VARIETIES

1. Pine or pine forest, or saffron milkcaps are wild mushrooms that are large (up to 20cm in diameter) and fleshy with orange caps. Remove the stalks and cook quickly at a high temperature.

Cepe, slippery jack or porcini mushrooms (*not pictured*) are large-topped, meaty mushrooms. They are mostly sold dried but can also be found fresh. If you have fresh mushrooms their strong flavour means you won't need many of them to spice up a risotto or stew. When found or bought fresh, they should be clean, firm and unmarked. Peel slippery jacks before cooking.

CULTIVATED VARIETIES

2. Button mushrooms or champignons are small with a cap tightly enclosing the stalk. They are very versatile and have a mild flavour. They can be stir-fried, grilled, cooked in soups and casseroles or served raw in salads. Buy those that are unblemished, with none of the gills showing, and with a stem that is very firmly attached to its cap. Use both stems and caps.

3. Cup mushrooms are slightly larger and darker in colour than the button, with their caps just starting to open. Cups have a distinctive flavour without being overpowering; they are perfect for soups, stir-fries and sauces, and are delicious sautéed with meat juices. Use both the stems and the caps.

4. Swiss brown, cremini or roman mushrooms have a mottled brown and white cap. The roman brown mushroom is slightly smaller than the swiss brown. These hold their shape well in cooking, so are suitable for casseroles or risottos, or marinated and served as an antipasti. Store on a tray in a single layer, covered with damp, absorbent paper and keep where cool air can circulate around them. Button or cup mushrooms can be substituted.

5. Portobello mushrooms Are just large swiss brown mushrooms. A dark-brown mushroom with full-bodied flavour, it is ideal for filling or barbecuing. Remove the dark gills from the underside of the mushroom cap with a spoon.

6. Flat or field mushrooms are intensely flavoured, larger and darker than button or cup mushrooms, and are very dense and meaty in texture. They are great filled and grilled, or fried and eaten as a vegetarian dish. Remove and discard the stems.

7. Shiitake mushrooms have an umbrella-like thick, spongy cap and a fibrous stem that should be discarded. It is better to cook shiitake than to eat them raw. Their rich, 'wild' flavour and filling meaty texture make them a perfect

mushroom to be braised then pan-fried and eaten on their own, or for flavouring broths and risottos; they also add texture to stir-fries and soups. Shiitakes will last for several days in the refrigerator in a porous paper bag.

8. Enoki mushrooms Bought in clumps of long, slender stems with tiny, snowy white caps, enokis have a delicate fruit flavour and a generally soft texture. Toss into a stir-fry at the last minute or add to an Asian-flavoured soup.

9. Oyster mushrooms are prized for their smooth texture and subtle, oyster-like flavour. The fan-shaped caps vary in colour from yellow to white to pink. They are delicate and

need very little cooking; are mainly used in light creamy sauces, risottos and omelettes, and go well with veal, seafood and poultry. Buy firm, smooth, unmarked mushrooms with a white base and a slightly anise-like aroma as these are an indication of freshness. They reduce considerably when cooked, so buy more than you think you'll need. Store in the refrigerator for up to 1 week, in a ventilated container to allow the air to circulate. Gently tear them, rather than chopping then with a knife.

10. Chestnut mushrooms With their small brown caps and long, thin white stems, chestnut mushrooms have a

strong, nutty flavour. They have a low moisture content so require slightly longer cooking than some other mushrooms. Trim the woody ends from the stems before use.

11. Shimeji are a Japanese variety also known as beech, hon-shimeji or pioppini. Colour ranges from white and yellow to tawny brown. The delicate flesh is sweet and suits stir-frying, pan-frying and steaming. Shimeji mushrooms have small flat caps with long, thick stems and are generally sold in clusters. Carefully separate mushrooms and remove from the base before use. Like other Asian varieties, shimeji tolerate only very short cooking times.

DRIED MUSHROOMS
Dried mushrooms need to be reconstituted in water before use. They retain almost all their flavour in the drying process, so it is a good choice for mushrooms that are not so readily available. Soak in hot water for about 30 minutes, depending on the size. Retain the soaking water for a stock or broth.

12. Chantarelles are a yellow, European mushroom with a soft, fruity taste.

13. Porcini are strongly-flavoured, meaty mushrooms.

Morels (*not pictured*) A richly-flavoured, cone-shaped mushroom having a honeycomb appearance.

Mixed oyster mushroom and ginger noodles

1 tablespoon peanut oil

2 cloves garlic, crushed

2cm piece fresh ginger (10g), grated

150g oyster mushrooms, chopped coarsely

150g pink oyster mushrooms, chopped coarsely

150g yellow oyster mushrooms, chopped coarsely

450g fresh thin rice noodles

⅓ cup (80ml) vegetarian mushroom oyster sauce

2 tablespoons lime juice

4 green onions, sliced thinly

1 Heat oil in wok; stir-fry garlic, ginger and mushrooms until mushrooms are almost tender.

2 Add noodles, sauce and juice; stir-fry until hot.

3 Divide noodles among bowls; serve sprinkled with onion.

prep & cook time 25 minutes **serves** 4

nutritional count per serving 5.6g total fat (0.9g saturated fat); 903kJ (216 cal); 0.9g carbohydrate; 7g protein; 6.1g fibre

Mushrooms are packed with nutrients and can be prepared in many ways, as either the star of the show, or in a smaller role within a meal. Mushrooms go well with herbs, butter, garlic, ginger, onion, cream or salty Asian sauces. They are great to stir-fry, roast, sauté or pan-fry, barbecue, or cook in a soup or risotto. You can also pickle or dry them to preserve seasonal varieties for later use. Mushrooms can be classified as cultivated or wild. Most cultivated mushrooms are available year round, though wild mushrooms are very seasonal. To enjoy the earthy flavour of wild mushrooms, you must wait for the perfect weather conditions. Some vendors at growers' markets will sometimes sell a limited supply of wild mushrooms when they have them. If you pick your own, have them checked by an expert before eating them as they may be poisonous.

CHOOSE mushrooms as described by variety. Avoid slimy looking caps and those that look shrivelled.

STORE mushrooms as described by variety, otherwise, store in a paper or calico bag in the refrigerator. They generally last for up to 3 days when stored in this way.

PREPARE by wiping over the mushrooms using a piece of damp absorbent paper. This removes any grit and prevents them becoming soggy. They become waterlogged if washed, making them difficult to sauté (they tend to steam in the pan and lose their beautiful flavour). Peeling mushrooms is time-consuming and unnecessary; many nutrients and much of the flavour is found in the skin.

DRY mushrooms by spreading them out and placing them in a sunny position until completely dry. This may take several days. Store them in an airtight container until ready to use.

Wild mushroom risotto

10g dried chantarelle mushrooms

10g dried porcini mushrooms

1 litre (4 cups) chicken or vegetable stock

2 cups (500ml) water

50g butter

100g chestnut mushrooms, trimmed

100g button mushrooms, sliced thickly

2 flat mushrooms (160g), halved, sliced thickly

4 shallots (100g), chopped finely

2 cloves garlic, crushed

2 cups (400g) arborio rice

½ cup (125ml) dry white wine

½ cup (40g) finely grated parmesan cheese

2 tablespoons finely chopped fresh chives

1 Combine chantarelle and porcini mushrooms, stock and the water in medium saucepan; bring to the boil. Reduce heat; simmer, covered.

2 Meanwhile, melt 30g of the butter in large saucepan; add remaining mushrooms to pan. Cook, stirring, until mushrooms are tender and liquid evaporates; remove from pan.

3 Melt remaining butter in same pan; cook shallots and garlic, stirring, until shallots soften. Add rice; stir to coat rice in butter mixture. Return mushrooms cooked in butter to pan with wine; bring to the boil. Reduce heat; simmer, uncovered, until liquid has almost evaporated. Add 1 cup simmering stock mixture; cook, stirring, over low heat, until stock is absorbed. Continue adding stock mixture, in 1 cup batches, stirring, until absorbed between additions. Total cooking time should be about 25 minutes or until rice is tender. Stir in cheese and chives.

serving idea Serve with a loaf of fresh crusty bread.

prep & cook time 40 minutes **serves** 4

nutritional count per serving 15.4g total fat (9.4g saturated fat); 2391kJ (572 cal); 82.2g carbohydrate; 17.9g protein; 4.4g fibre

Onions & garlic

The strong, distinctive flavours of onion and garlic make them among the most indispensable flavours of the cooking world. Onion forms the basis of innumerable recipes, providing depth, complexity and flavour, while garlic is a basic ingredient in many classic Italian, French and Asian recipes. Cooking both onion and garlic smooths out the flavour, making them more mild, and bringing out their natural sweetness. Onions can be broadly grouped into 'dry' and 'green' onions. Dry onions are mature onions with a papery skin. These last for months. Green onions are simply immature onions – although there are several varieties – they are moist and relatively mild and last up to a week in the refrigerator.

2.

1.

4.

8.

3.

VARIETIES

1. White onions are slightly more moist than brown onions and, though strong in flavour, are less sharp than brown onions, so are great thinly sliced in salads.

2. Brown onions become very sweet when roasted and are delicious with roasted meat.

3. Red, or spanish onions have a moderate sweetness when cooked. Caramelised red onion has a sticky, jammy texture, perfect with soft cheese or red meat.

4. Pickling, or baby onions, are literally any variety of early harvest onion. They usually weigh around 25g each. They can be pickled, cooked whole in a stew, or roasted to release their delicate sweet flavour.

5. Shallots, or french shallots, eschalots or golden shallots, are small and elongated with brown skin and pale purple flesh. They grow in tight clusters, like garlic, and are particularly integral to French cooking.

6. Spring onions are immature onions with a semi-developed bulb. The green tops can be used in soups, stir-fries and salads while the white part gives a stronger onion flavour.

7. Green onions are often incorrectly called shallots, and in America, scallions. Milder than spring onions, green onions are immature onions with an unformed bulb. The hottest part of the onion is the white part; the flavour mellows the higher up the green shoot you get.

8. Garlic grows underground, and usually has about 12 to 15 cloves in each bulb. It is dried before being sold.

CHOOSE dry onions with papery skin and no sprouts. Green onions should be crisp and wet-looking, but not slimy. Garlic should be hard when squeezed, with no sprouts or mouldy patches.

STORE dry onions and garlic in a cool, dark, dry place with freely circulating air. They will keep for at least one month if stored in this way, although brown onions will last longer than white onions. Once cut or peeled, onions deteriorate rapidly. Cover them in plastic wrap and keep them in the refrigerator for up to 2 days. To store green onions, discard about the top third of the stems then cut off the root ends, pulling back and removing any loose skin-like layers. Wrap onions in absorbent paper and place in an airtight plastic bag; refrigerate until ready to use. Use within 2 days.

PREPARE Before chopping or slicing, soak onions in iced water for 30 to 60 minutes to slow the release of the enzyme that causes the nose and eyes to sting and water. This also hydrates the onion skin, making it easier to peel. To chop onions, cut off the top end then slice through the centre lengthways toward the root; discard the skin, keeping the root end intact. Place onion half flat on a board. Grip with one hand

and, using a sharp knife, slice, first down the length then across, in a crosshatch pattern. Discard the root end. Remove the roots and any discoloured tops from green onions, peel off any coarse-looking outside layers, then slice or chop as required. To easily peel garlic for chopping, place a single clove on a chopping board. Press down on it with the flat side of a large, heavy knife using the heel of your hand. The skin comes away easily. Scatter with a little salt and chop roughly – this makes pulping the clove easier.

RAW onions can be sliced finely and used in salads or tossed through pasta; red or white onions are best for this.

STIR-FRY sliced or quartered onions for 1 to 3 minutes; they should retain a slightly crunchy texture.

SWEAT onions for a smooth, sweet base to a pie or tart filling, risotto, stew or soup. Cook them very slowly in the smallest amount of butter, oil, or stock, covered, over a low heat so that the fibres of the vegetable break down.

SAUTÉ/PAN-FRY Onions have a high sugar content. When cooked and the sugar is heated, it first melts, making the onion soft and translucent, then changes colour. As it caramelises, the flavour becomes more rich, intense and fragrant. This works particularly well with brown and red onions. Cook slowly in olive oil over a low heat until the onion is softened, then add a little brown sugar and balsamic vinegar and continue cooking for about 15 minutes or until sticky and a deep brown or purple colour. Caramelised onion has myriad uses – try using it in pies, tarts, sandwiches or pizza. It can also accompany pâté, cheese or steak.

DEEP-FRY Dip onion rings in batter or egg then crumbs, then deep-fry until browned for an American-style treat. Deep-fry (use a little oil in a deep pan) pieces of spring or green onion – take care as they spit when frying – and sprinkle them over the top of Asian meals

ROAST onions and garlic to take the sharpness and strength out of the taste and to soften the texture. Both garlic and onions infuse flavour to whatever they are roasted with.

RAW garlic is also often tossed through pasta or salads, or used in a sauce such as aïoli or pesto. Uncooked garlic has a very strong flavour and can be quite 'hot'.

BLANCH and puree garlic for a milder garlic flavour to mix with butter, then spread on toast, mix through pasta or blanched vegetables, or rub over chicken or meat before cooking. Bring cold water with the unpeeled garlic to a simmer, drain off the hot water and repeat twice. The garlic will peel easily and can then be pureed.

STIR-FRY minced garlic with any fragrant spices as the base for a stir-fry. Make sure the oil is hot before you add the garlic, and keep it moving to prevent it from burning. Quartered onion can be added next, before other ingredients.

SAUTÉ/PAN-FRY Never fry garlic until it is black as it is inedible when fried to that point. French and Italian chefs advise cooking garlic only until fragrant, and never browned, although in Asian cooking, deep-frying garlic is a common practice.

Roasted balsamic onions

2 medium red onions
  (340g), quartered
2 medium brown onions
  (300g), quartered
2 bulbs garlic, halved
  horizontally
2 tablespoons olive oil
1 tablespoon
  balsamic vinegar
1 tablespoon brown sugar

1 Preheat oven to 220°C/200°C fan-forced.
2 Combine ingredients in medium baking dish.
3 Roast, brushing occasionally with pan juices, about
 40 minutes or until onions and garlic are tender
and caramelised.

prep & cook time 1 hour serves 4
nutritional count per serving 9.8g total fat
(1.4g saturated fat); 702kJ (168 cal);
13.9g carbohydrate; 3.5g protein; 5.6g fibre

Parsnips

Parsnips are a slightly fleshy, herb-flavoured root vegetable, very similar to carrots. They are sweet and have a wonderfully rich flavour. They are a cold weather vegetable, and add a fresh flavour to stews and roasts. Parsnip goes very well with strongly-flavoured red meat.

CHOOSE parsnips that are of even colour and aren't too large. Very large parsnips can have a woody core so avoid them.

STORE in the refrigerator. They will last up to a week.

PREPARE by cutting off the top and tail then peeling with a vegetable peeler.

ROAST parsnips that have been sliced in half lengthways. Toss in olive oil or add to the pan with the roasting meat. Roast at 200°C/180°C fan-forced for about 40 minutes then test for tenderness.

STEAM parsnips for about 8 minutes.

BOIL parsnips, covered, in only enough water to cover for about 8 minutes.

MICROWAVE Parsnips are suitable to be cooked in a microwave oven.

PUREE or mash steamed, boiled or microwaved parsnip with butter, cream or simply a little vegetable stock, season with ground nutmeg or crushed cumin or coriander seeds for a silky sweet bed for lamb backstraps.

Roasted caramelised parsnips

1kg parsnips, halved
  lengthways
2 tablespoons olive oil
¼ cup (55g) brown sugar
1 teaspoon ground nutmeg
1 tablespoon finely chopped
  fresh flat-leaf parsley

1 Preheat oven to 220°C/200°C fan-forced.
2 Combine parsnip, oil, sugar and nutmeg in large baking dish; roast about 1 hour or until parsnip is browned and tender.
3 Serve parsnip sprinkled with parsley.

prep & cook time 1 hour 10 minutes **serves** 4
nutritional count per serving 9.6g total fat (1.3g saturated fat); 1074kJ (257 cal); 35.8g carbohydrate; 4.1g protein; 5.7g fibre

Peas

VARIETIES

1. Green peas Little, sweet parcels of nutrients that explode in your mouth, green peas are the epitome of spring. Because frozen peas are available year round, people forget how fantastic fresh peas are in spring. As a guide, for 1 cup (260g) of shelled fresh peas, you will need to buy about 400g of peas in their pods.

Baby green peas (*not pictured*) are simply immature peas. They are sweeter and, because they are smaller, they tend to suit some recipes better than the larger more mature peas.

2. Sugar snap peas are eaten whole (pod and peas). The pod is fat and short with a thick, sweet and very crunchy wall. The peas inside are small but larger than those in a snow pea. Blanch, eat raw or toss into a stir-fry.

3. Snow peas, or mange-tout, are also eaten whole. The pod is thin-walled, flat and broad with small seeds. They are crunchy and sweet, and are beautiful raw or blanched.

4. Snow pea sprouts are the delicate immature sprouts that are harvested before the pea pods begin to grow. They are crisp and watery with a fresh tasting, small leaf at the top.

5. Snow pea tendrils are the leaves and the elegant, fine and curly tendrils of the snow pea vine, harvested when more mature than at sprout harvesting time. Tendrils are usually only bought in large plastic packages, making it hard to use them all before they deteriorate.

CHOOSE green, waxy looking peas that aren't too mottled or have any bulges. The younger the fresh peas are, the better, so don't buy any that are too large. Avoid sprouts and tendrils that look yellowed or wilted.

STORE snow peas and sugar snap peas in the refrigerator for up to 2 days; green peas, snow pea tendrils and sprouts are best eaten on the day of purchase, but may last a day longer in the refrigerator.

PREPARE snow peas and sugar snap peas by cutting off the tops and tails and stripping back the strings that run down the edges. To pod green peas, make an incision very close to the top then snap peas open. Run your thumb or finger down the closed edge of the pod and the peas will pop out.

RAW and crunchy snow peas, snow pea tendrils and sprouts can be added to a 'salad' of fresh, boiled peas and corn kernels. Snow pea tendrils and sprouts add fabulous texture to an egg sandwich, crunch to a salad and make an excellent garnish for soup.

BOIL Add green peas to boiling water; boil, covered, about 4 minutes or until tender.

BLANCH snow peas and sugar snap peas for 2 minutes in boiling water until changed in colour to bright green.

STEAM fresh green peas, sugar snap peas and snow peas for up to 3 minutes.

MICROWAVE Peas are suitable to be cooked in a microwave oven. Snow peas and sugar snap peas will take a little less time than fresh green peas.

Once cooked, drain peas immediately then plunge into a bowl of cold water to arrest the cooking. Dress green peas with butter and chopped fresh mint, salt and pepper.

STIR-FRY snow peas, snow pea sprouts and sugar snap peas for 1 to 3 minutes. Stir-fry snow pea sprouts with garlic and ginger for about 2 minutes to make a delicious topping for salmon or trout.

PUREE cooked peas with a little butter and dollop onto toasted fresh crusty bread or alongside meat, chicken or fish.

FROZEN peas are an excellent substitute when fresh peas are unavailable or podding them is too time consuming. If using them in a hot mixture, such as a pie mixture, risotto or soup, simply stir them frozen into the mix; the heat from the cooking food will defrost the peas. Otherwise, to defrost, splash with a little water and microwave for 1 minute, or blanch in boiling water for 1 minute or until tender.

Peas with mint butter

2¼ cups (350g) fresh shelled peas
40g butter, softened
1 tablespoon finely chopped fresh mint
1 teaspoon finely grated lemon rind

1 Boil, steam or microwave peas until tender; drain.
2 Meanwhile, combine remaining ingredients in small bowl.
3 Serve peas topped with butter mixture.
prep & cook time 10 minutes **serves** 4
nutritional count per serving 8.6g total fat (5.4g saturated fat); 589kJ (141 cal); 8.6g carbohydrate; 5.2g protein; 5g fibre
tip You need approximately 1kg fresh pea pods to get the required amount of shelled peas needed for this recipe.

Potatoes

MASHING VARIETIES

King edward (*not pictured*) are plump and rosy skinned. They are fluffy and creamy when mashed.

1. Spunta have a yellow flesh and a floury texture. They are also great fried.

2. Purple congo A sweet tasting potato, with a purple, floury flesh. Can also be sliced into lengths and fried for chips.

3. Dutch cream A truly luxurious potato; so creamy, smooth and sweet that this potato needs nothing but a little salt when mashed for absolutely delicious results. High in starch so when pureed it is like smooth creamy butter.

FIRM VARIETIES

4. Baby new potato, or chat, are early harvest potatoes with a thin pale skin. Good for steaming, then tossed in butter and herbs and eaten hot or in a salad as they hold their shape well. No need to peel unless required for your recipe.

5. Kipfler A small, elongated knobbly potato with a nutty flavour. Scrub then roast or boil, steam or microwave. Also used mashed, baked or in salads.

6. Pinkeye Roast or boil and use in salads. This waxy, purple-blushed potato has a chestnut-like flavour.

7. Pontiac has a strong potato flavour, pink skin with deep eyes and white flesh. It is good for boiling and is especially good for roasting. Mashed pontiacs have a firm body, making it a good choice as an accompaniment to a meat dish with sauce.

8. Bintje has a creamy skin and yellow flesh. Bintjes are good for roasting, frying and in salads.
Pink fir apple (*not pictured*) has a waxy flesh that stands up well to roasting or boiling then eating while hot or adding cold to a salad.

ALL–ROUNDER VARIETIES
9. Desiree This oval-shaped potato has a waxy, yellow flesh. Desiree boils well and can be mashed and used for mopping up gravy. It is also good roasted.
10. Sebago are good for frying, roasting or mashing.
11. Royal blue has a purple skin with yellow flesh and a buttery flavour. Good for mashing, roasting or frying.

12. Russet burbank, or Idaho, are excellent roasted or fried. It can also be mashed.
Coliban (*not pictured*) A crumbly potato; take care not to overboil as it may fall apart – don't use in a stew or soup. A good mashing and roasting potato.
Nicola (*not pictured*) has a buttery, sweet flavour. Can be roasted, boiled or steamed but is best used for mashing. Has a good dry texture well suited to making gnocchi.

The humble potato needs no introduction, but the amazing varieties now available to the consumer do. Once just 'old' (any dirty potato, mostly sebago) and 'new' (clean, pale-skinned waxy potatoes) varieties were on offer, but now there is a particular potato suited to every taste and purpose. Inexpensive, easy to grow and store and high in energy, it is no wonder potatoes are enjoyed in vast quantities in nearly every cuisine around the world. The common varieties are available year round while the lesser known varieties are available in winter only.

CHOOSE very firm, heavy potatoes that feel dry and have no sprouting eyes or green spots. Any potato with green spots should be avoided as this may indicate that the potato harbours toxins produced by over-exposure to sunlight. They also taste bitter. Although potatoes with deep eyes can have a better flavour, try to pick those that have smooth skin for ease of peeling.

STORE in a cool, dark, dry place for up to 3 weeks. 'New' potatoes – those that have a clean, pale thin skin last only a few days.

PREPARE Wash dirty potatoes well before you cook them. If peeling, remove the eyes with the tip of the vegetable peeler using a twisting action. Potatoes brown as their flesh is exposed to air, so drop them straight into water as you go. Chop into large chunks if you are boiling or steaming for mash or gnocchi batter as they will cook more quickly that way.

BOIL potatoes using enough cold water to barely cover the potatoes in the saucepan. Sprinkle a little salt into the pan and cook with the lid on until potatoes are tender when tested with a sharp knife. Quartered potatoes will take about 15 minutes to cook.

STEAM potato chunks for about 20 minutes. Steaming is the best method if cooking potatoes for gnocchi as water absorption is less, allowing for a dryer, fluffier gnocchi.

MICROWAVE whole unpeeled potatoes then halve and cook on the barbecue, or cut into wedges then roast, or leave whole for stuffing. Prick the skin of unpeeled potatoes well with a fork.

Use cooked potatoes in a salad or proceed with a recipe for roast or mashed potato, chips, wedges, rösti or gnocchi.

DEEP-FRY for chips by cutting uncooked, peeled potato into 1cm chips. Stand in a large bowl of cold water, about 30 minutes to prevent discolouration. Drain and pat dry with absorbent paper. Heat oil (we like peanut oil best), in deep pan until hot (see page 113). Deep-fry chips, in batches, until they are tender, but not browned. Drain on absorbent paper; stand 10 minutes. Reheat oil; deep-fry chips, in batches, until golden brown. Drain on absorbent paper.

ROAST potatoes after partly cooking by steaming, boiling or microwaving. Roughen the edges slightly by shaking them in a colander, dry them with absorbent paper, then roast, brushed with a little olive oil, at 200°C/180°C fan-forced, about 1 hour or until browned. Whole, unpeeled potatoes (rubbed with oil and sprinkled with sea salt, if you like) can be roasted for about an hour at the same temperature. The skin will become crisp and puffy.

SAUTÉ Cut potatoes into 1cm slices. Heat oil or butter, or a little of both in a frying pan; cook potato, covered, tossing occasionally, about 15 minutes or until browned.

Potato and rosemary pizza

1 cup (250ml) warm water
1 teaspoon caster sugar
8g sachet dried yeast
2½ cups (375g) plain flour
1 teaspoon coarse cooking salt
2 tablespoons olive oil
400g baby new potatoes, sliced thinly
1 clove garlic, crushed
1 tablespoon coarsely chopped fresh rosemary

1 Combine the water, sugar and yeast in small jug. Stand in warm place about 10 minutes or until frothy.
2 Sift flour and salt into large bowl, add yeast mixture; mix to a soft dough. Knead dough on floured surface about 10 minutes or until smooth and elastic. Place dough in lightly greased large bowl; cover. Stand in warm place about 1 hour or until doubled in size.
3 Preheat oven to 220°C/200°C fan-forced. Grease two oven trays.
4 Divide dough in half. Roll each portion into 18cm x 30cm rectangles; place on trays. Brush pizza bases with half the oil.
5 Combine potatoes, garlic, rosemary and remaining oil in medium bowl; layer potato mixture evenly over bases.
6 Bake pizzas about 30 minutes or until browned.
prep & cook time 45 minutes (+ standing) **serves** 6
nutritional count per serving 7g total fat (1g saturated fat); 1367kJ (327 cal); 54.5g carbohydrate; 8.9g protein; 4.1g fibre

Potato bake

1kg sebago potatoes, cut into 5mm-thick slices
2 teaspoons olive oil
1 medium brown onion (150g), sliced thinly
6 slices pancetta (90g), chopped coarsely
1 cup (250ml) cream
½ cup (120g) sour cream
2 tablespoons finely chopped fresh chives
1 cup (120g) coarsely grated cheddar cheese

1 Preheat oven to 200°C/180°C fan-forced. Grease 2 litre
(8 cup) ovenproof dish.
2 Boil, steam or microwave potato until tender; drain.
3 Meanwhile, heat oil in medium frying pan; cook onion and
pancetta, stirring, until onion softens and pancetta is crisp.
4 Combine cream, sour cream and chives in medium jug.
5 Layer a third of the potato slices over base of dish; sprinkle
with half the pancetta mixture. Pour a third of the cream mixture
over pancetta mixture; sprinkle with a third of the cheese.
Repeat layering, finishing with cheese.
6 Bake, uncovered, in oven, about 30 minutes or until browned.
Stand 10 minutes before serving.
prep & cook time 45 minutes serves 6
nutritional count per serving 36.5g total fat
(22.4g saturated fat); 1956kJ (468 cal);
21.8g carbohydrate; 13g protein; 2.6g fibre

Hasselback potatoes

4 medium desiree potatoes (800g), halved horizontally
40g butter, melted
2 tablespoons olive oil
¼ cup (25g) packaged breadcrumbs
½ cup (60g) finely grated cheddar cheese

1 Preheat oven to 180°C/160°C fan-forced.
2 Place one potato half, cut-side down, on chopping board;
place a chopstick on board along each side of potato. Slice
potato thinly, cutting through to chopsticks to prevent cutting
all the way through. Repeat with remaining potato halves.
3 Coat potatoes in combined butter and oil in medium baking
dish; place, rounded-side up, in single layer. Roast 1 hour,
brushing frequently with oil mixture.
4 Sprinkle combined breadcrumbs and cheese over potatoes;
roast about 10 minutes or until browned.
prep & time 1 hour 30 minutes serves 4
nutritional count per serving 22.8g total fat
(10g saturated fat); 1463kJ (350 cal);
24.5g carbohydrate; 8.8g protein; 3g fibre

Warm kipfler potato salad

1kg kipfler potatoes, halved lengthways
¼ cup (60ml) olive oil
1 teaspoon finely grated lemon rind
1 tablespoon lemon juice
2 teaspoons wholegrain mustard
1 small red onion (100g), sliced thinly
1 cup loosely packed fresh flat-leaf parsley

1 Boil, steam or microwave potato until tender; drain.
2 Whisk oil, rind, juice and mustard in large bowl; mix in potatoes, onion and parsley.
prep & cook time 30 minutes **serves** 4
nutritional count per serving 14g total fat
(1.9g saturated fat); 1267kJ (303 cal);
34.4g carbohydrate; 6.8g protein; 6.2g fibre

Perfect mashed potato

1kg spunta potatoes, chopped coarsely
40g butter
¾ cup (180ml) hot milk

1 Boil, steam or microwave potatoes until tender; drain.
2 Using the back of a wooden spoon; push potato through fine sieve into large bowl. Stir in butter and milk.
prep & cook time 30 minutes **serves** 4
nutritional count per serving 10.2g total fat
(6.6g saturated fat); 1028kJ (246 cal);
30.1g carbohydrate; 6.7g protein; 3.4g fibre
tip Using hot milk instead of cold gives a creamier mash.

Pumpkins

1.

4.

5.

1.

3.

4.

2.

VARIETIES

1. Jarrahdale is a sweet-fleshed pumpkin. Its blue-grey ridged skin is easier to cut than some of the other varieties.

2. Butternut has a sweet, nutty flavour and a fairly dry texture, which makes this one of the most versatile pumpkins. It is good for everything from soups to roasting.

3. Jap pumpkin is very sweet and nutty, with a soft, dry flesh that melts in your mouth when cooked. Well-suited to roasting with the skin on.

4. Golden nugget is a small, round pumpkin with golden-yellow flesh that is milder in flavour than some other varieties. It has a lot of seeds, and a good shape, which makes it the perfect stuffing pumpkin.

5. Queensland Blue is a full-flavoured pumpkin with a blue-grey, ridged skin. These are the best pumpkins to use in pumpkin scones.

Pumpkin is available all year. It is one of the most versatile vegetables; firm enough to sauté or stew, yet soft enough when cooked to be able to be blended to a fine puree. It is sweetly savoury, making it an equally suitable addition to either a roast dinner or a sweet pie. It has a high liquid absorption rate, so dry methods of cooking are best to prevent soggy results. Pumpkin is used in many cuisines: try cooking it with cumin or nutmeg, cream or coconut milk, ricotta cheese, chilli, garlic and rosemary, cinnamon, pulses, curry or red meat.

CHOOSE heavy pumpkins. If already cut, look for moist-looking surfaces

STORE uncut pumpkin in a cool, dark, dry place. Uncut, they will last for weeks. Cut pumpkin is inclined to mould and should be stored, with the seeds and stringy sections of the hollow removed, wrapped in plastic wrap in the crisper section of the refrigerator for up to 2 days.

PREPARE Peeling pumpkin is one of the more dangerous kitchen activities, so do so with care. Cut a section with a large, heavy knife. Then place it on the cut side for stability and, cutting away from you, cut the skin off. If you intend to boil, steam or microwave your pumpkin, cut it into chunks and peel it after cooking it for a few minutes, when the flesh and skin has softened slightly. Roast pumpkin doesn't need to be peeled, as when roasted, the skin is soft, edible and tasty – especially jap and butternut pumpkins.

BOIL pieces of pumpkin, covered, in as little water as possible to avoid waterlogged results. Medium-sized pieces will take about 8 minutes to cook.

STEAM for about 20 minutes.

MICROWAVE Pumpkin is suitable for cooking in a microwave oven.

STIR-FRY finely sliced pumpkin for 3 to 5 minutes.

GRILL OR BARBECUE thin slices until tender for a char-grilled flavour that is great with barbecued lamb or beef, or in a salad with a light dressing.

ROAST chunks of pumpkin at 200°C/180°C fan-forced for 45 minutes to 1 hour or until tender and brown. Roast pumpkin can also be mashed, pureed with vegetable stock to make a rich, thick soup, added to a salad, or served with some greens and red meat for a classic Sunday roast.

PUREED or MASHED pumpkin is delicious as it is, but can be used in sweet pies, custards, scones, for gnocchi, or as a filling for fresh ravioli.

TO STUFF small pumpkins, particularly golden nuggets, slice the top quarter off the pumpkin (the 'lid') and scrape out the seeds and stringy bits. Place the stuffing into the cavity and bake the pumpkin and lid at 180°C/160°C fan-forced for about 45 minutes or until tender.
Pumpkins are great stuffed with a cheesy, creamy filling, or try a mixture of cooked onion and rice with a few herbs and some dried fruit and seeds.

ADD to a casserole, stew or curry to give it depth and sweetness.

Spiced pumpkin soup with cinnamon cream

1 tablespoon olive oil

1 medium brown onion (150g), chopped coarsely

1 clove garlic, crushed

2 teaspoons ground cumin

½ teaspoon ground coriander

1kg butternut pumpkin, chopped coarsely

2 medium potatoes (400g), chopped coarsely

2 cups (500ml) water

1½ cups (375ml) vegetable stock

5cm strip orange rind

cinnamon cream

⅔ cup (160ml) cream

½ teaspoon ground cinnamon

1 Heat oil in large saucepan; cook onion and garlic, stirring, until onion softens. Add spices; cook, stirring, until fragrant. Add pumpkin, potato, the water, stock and rind; bring to the boil. Reduce heat; simmer, covered, 20 minutes or until vegetables are tender.

2 Meanwhile, make cinnamon cream.

3 Blend or process soup, in batches, until smooth. Return soup to same pan; stir over heat until heated through.

4 Serve bowls of soup topped with cinnamon cream.

cinnamon cream Beat ingredients in small bowl with electric mixer until soft peaks form.

prep & cook time 30 minutes **serves** 4

nutritional count per serving 23.2g total fat (12.9g saturated fat); 1530kJ (366 cal); 28.6g carbohydrate; 8.8g protein; 4.5g fibre

1.

2.

Radishes

VARIETIES

1. Red radish has a peppery mustard taste, however, very pungent radishes are increasingly difficult to find. The flesh is white, crisp and moist with a clean taste. It is surprisingly versatile, too, though usually eaten raw or pickled, it can also be cooked. Long radishes are difficult to find, but usually have a little more heat than the small globes.

2. Daikon is an Asian radish that is relatively mild and slightly sweet. It can be used raw as an accompaniment to sashimi or in a salad, or cooked, in Asian soups, stir-fries or sweet and sour dishes. It is white both on the inside and out and has a texture similar to unripe pear.

Radishes and daikon are root vegetables, related to the turnip and swede. They belong to the mustard family, which accounts for their peppery flavour. Taste before using, as the degree of heat can vary between radishes from very hot to very mild. Cooking reduces the heat of radishes and daikon and brings out their natural sweetness. Radishes grow quickly so they are a great vegetable for kids to grow in the garden, as they get very quick results. Radishes and daikon go well with ginger, orange, fresh herbs, cabbage and salad leaves.

CHOOSE radishes that are bright with fresh green leaves and daikon that are unblemished and not too large.

STORE unwashed radishes and daikon in the crisper section of the refrigerator for up to a week.

PREPARE Radishes do not need to be peeled, just remove the green tops then wash and proceed with your recipe. Prepare daikon by cutting off the tail and leaves; peel then cut as required for the recipe. Julienne for a stir fry or cube and add to a casserole or soup.

RAW Slice radishes or daikon thinly for a salad, shred into ribbons for a garnish or add thin slices to buttered bread for a delicious sandwich fit for a tea party.

BRAISE chopped radishes in stock until tender for a vegetable accompaniment.

STIR-FRY Julienned daikon should be stir-fried for no more than 1 minute to allow it to cook without losing its fresh crunch.

PICKLE daikon for an accompaniment to almost any Asian meal, especially sashimi (a raw fish dish).

Fattoush

2 large pitta bread (160g)
⅓ cup (80ml) olive oil
2 tablespoons lemon juice
1 clove garlic, crushed
3 red radishes (105g), trimmed, sliced thinly
½ small daikon (200g), grated coarsely
2 medium tomatoes (300g), chopped coarsely
1 lebanese cucumber (130g), chopped coarsely
1 small red onion (100g), sliced thinly
1 small green capsicum (150g), chopped coarsely
1 cup loosely packed fresh mint leaves
1 cup loosely packed fresh flat-leaf parsley leaves

1 Preheat grill to hot.
2 Place bread on oven tray; grill until crisp. Break bread into pieces.
3 Whisk oil, juice and garlic together in large bowl. Mix in half the bread and remaining ingredients.
4 Serve fattoush sprinkled with remaining bread.
prep & cook time 20 minutes **serves** 4
nutritional count per serving 19.7g total fat (2.7g saturated fat); 1367kJ (327 cal); 28.1g carbohydrate; 6.8g protein; 5.8g fibre

Salad greens

VARIETIES

1. Iceberg lettuce is crisp and refreshing with a watery crunch. Best eaten when absolutely fresh, iceberg has a very simple taste, allowing it to mix well with a great variety of flavours and textures. Used as the cups in sang choy bow, in a simple crunchy salad, with hard-boiled eggs in a sandwich, or in a summery cool lettuce soup.

2. Butter and mignonette lettuce have soft leaves and a soft flavour, making them delicate all-rounders. A very faint bitterness makes them an ideal base for almost any dressing. Butter lettuce, which is green, is the better known, and mignonette is tinged with red.

3. Cos and baby cos lettuce are best known for their appearance in a caesar salad; they have a crisp spine and neutral-tasting leaves. The scooping shape of the cos lettuce and its softly crinkled leaves make it perfect for laying carefully in a salad bowl or platter to capture a creamy dressing. Remove the tough outer leaves from the larger lettuce. You don't generally need to remove outer leaves from baby cos; simply remove the root and core before use.

4. Red and green oak lettuce are tender and mildly-flavoured with curly, floppy leaves that are also found in a mesclun salad mix. The white stems 'rust' when cut with a knife so snapping them off at the core, one at a time, is better.

Radicchio (*not pictured*) has red, bitter leaves that can be eaten raw in a salad, or lightly grilled. Its refreshing bite is enhanced by salty accompaniments, such as blue cheese, which balances the bitterness. Add to pasta for a sharp bite and some colour.

5. Radicchio treviso is one of many varieties of radicchio; the treviso is named after its place of origin in Italy, and is a long-headed version of normal radicchio.

6. Mizuna is a Japanese leaf, similar in size and shape to baby rocket leaves. Its sharply jagged and aromatic leaves have a mild-mustard taste, which are a treat when tossed with a Japanese-flavoured or miso-based dressing.

7. Rocket and baby rocket, are also known as roquette, rugula, arugula and rucola. Baby rocket, also known as wild rocket, is sharply peppery. Rocket is best eaten young, as it becomes very hot and grassy in flavour when mature. The peppery flavour marries well with char-grilled food, so a rocket salad goes great with barbecued foods. Pair it with other strong flavours, such as balsamic vinegar and mature cheese. It does not last long in the refrigerator, so buy only enough to eat that day. Only wash leaves just before using.

8. Red and green coral lettuce is smallish with a mild, slightly bitter taste and tightly crinkled, soft leaves that help trap light, oil-based dressings.

9. Watercress is a pretty salad leaf and is good either as a garnish or in a mixed salad. It has a mustard flavour with a fresh crunch to the stems that adds a delicious texture when used in a sandwich, especially an egg sandwich. Trim before using, leaving 2cm to 3cm of the stem and the leaves. Lemon juice, nut oils, such as macadamia or walnut are good accompaniments for watercress.

Tatsoi, or rosette buk choy, (*pictured page 10*) is discussed further in the Asian Greens chapter (*see page 11*). Young, soft tatsoi leaves are often eaten as a salad green. Larger, tougher pieces are chopped and cooked.

Witlof or belgian endive (*not pictured*) as it's known in the US, or chicory (UK) is discussed more thoroughly in the witlof chapter (*see page 106*). It is a popular, mildly bitter, crunchy salad green. Choose witlof that are as pale as possible within the white sections.

10. Curly endive belongs to the same family as witlof, and also has a bitter tang to its leaves. Its shaggy sprigs have a grassy freshness that goes well with roast beetroot or creamy dressings.

11. Baby spinach leaf tastes much like the mature spinach but is a little less tart. Baby spinach in a salad is a fabulous way to get your daily dose of Popeye energy. Choose dark green, crisp leaves and eat on the day you buy them.

Chicory (*not pictured*) has long, dark leaves with ragged edges; it can be used as a salad green, or cooked in a pan until wilted then eaten as a side dish. Its faintly bitter taste mellows when grilled. Look for bright, crisp leaves.

12. Maiche or lamb's lettuce has small, tender, velvety leaves with a sweet, slightly nutty, flavour. It is available in the cooler months and is sold in punnets. The leaves should be deep green, with no yellow tinge, and should look velvety. It is very fragile, so handle with care. Add to a salad and toss gently with a light dressing, or add to a soup or omelette and cook briefly. Combine with creamy avocado and fresh sweet ingredients, such as apple, tomato, peas or grapes.

13. Mesclun salad is a combination of a variety of baby greens. There are often tired pieces residing in a mesclun mix, so buy more than you need and discard these, or mix your own mesclun.

A basic salad of fresh, tender leaves dressed in a simple vinaigrette is an absolute winner and goes with almost any meal. With a few select additions it becomes a meal on its own. Salad leaves can generally be divided into those with soft, fresh-tasting leaves, those with bitter leaves or those with peppery-mustard leaves. Choose an appropriate dressing for the type of leaves you have. Bitter leaves match well with a salty or sharp dressing, peppery leaves suit grilled foods and strong flavours such as vinegar. Soft leaves support almost any kind of dressing.

CHOOSE fresh, moist-looking leaves that do not look limp or pale in colour.

STORE Most salad leaves have a very short shelf life and are particularly delicate. In almost all cases, it is best to eat them on the day you buy them for the tastiest results. Store leaves in the refrigerator, unwashed, and eat them as soon as possible.

PREPARE To wash, plunge into cold water, remove immediately, then dry gently in a salad spinner or pat dry with a clean towel.

Baby cos caesar salad

1 small french bread stick (150g), sliced thinly
¼ cup (60ml) olive oil
4 slices prosciutto (60g)
4 eggs
2 baby cos lettuce (360g), leaves separated
1 cup (80g) flaked parmesan cheese
caesar dressing
2 egg yolks
1 clove garlic, quartered
4 drained anchovy fillets
2 tablespoons lemon juice
2 teaspoons dijon mustard
½ cup (125ml) olive oil
1 tablespoon warm water, approximately

1 Preheat oven to 180°C/160°C fan-forced.
2 Make caesar dressing.
3 Combine bread and oil in medium bowl; toast bread on oven tray until croûtons are browned lightly.
4 Meanwhile, cook prosciutto in heated large frying pan until crisp; drain on absorbent paper, chop coarsely.
5 Poach eggs until the whites are set but the yolks are still runny.
6 Combine lettuce, cheese, croûtons, prosciutto and dressing in large bowl; divide among serving bowls. Serve topped with poached eggs.
caesar dressing Blend or process egg yolks, garlic, anchovies, juice and mustard until smooth. With motor operating, gradually add oil, in a thin steady stream; blend until dressing thickens. Add as much of the warm water as required to thin dressing.
prep & cook time 30 minutes **serves** 4
nutritional count per serving 54.2g total fat (11.5g saturated fat); 2809kJ (672 cal); 22.2g carbohydrate; 23.6g protein; 3.5g fibre

Salad Dressings

Lemon and macadamia dressing

½ cup (125ml) macadamia oil

⅓ cup (45g) finely chopped roasted macadamia nuts

2 teaspoons finely grated lemon rind

2 tablespoons lemon juice

1 teaspoon caster sugar

1 Whisk ingredients in small jug until combined.

prep time 10 minutes

makes 1 cup

nutritional count per tablespoon 12.4g total fat (1.8g saturated fat); 477kJ (114 cal); 0.6g carbohydrate; 0.3g protein; 0.2g fibre

Honey mustard dressing

½ cup (150g) mayonnaise

¼ cup (60ml) cider vinegar

1 tablespoon honey

2 teaspoons wholegrain mustard

1 Whisk ingredients in small jug until combined.

prep time 5 minutes

makes 1 cup

nutritional count per tablespoon 4.1g total fat (0.5g saturated fat); 230kJ (55 cal); 4.5g carbohydrate; 0.2g protein; 0.1g fibre

Asian dressing

¼ cup (60ml) peanut oil
¼ cup (60ml) rice vinegar
2 tablespoons light soy sauce
1 tablespoon lime juice
1 clove garlic, crushed
2cm piece fresh ginger
   (10g), grated
1 fresh small red thai chilli,
   chopped finely
1 tablespoon finely chopped
   fresh coriander
1 tablespoon finely
   chopped fresh mint

1 Combine ingredients in
screw-top jar; shake well.
prep time 10 minutes
makes 1 cup
**nutritional count per
tablespoon** 4.6g total fat
(0.8g saturated fat); 176kJ
(42 cal); 0.2g carbohydrate;
0.3g protein; 0.1g fibre

French dressing

⅓ cup (80ml)
   white wine vinegar
2 teaspoons dijon mustard
1 teaspoon caster sugar
⅔ cup (160ml) olive oil

1 Whisk vinegar, mustard
and sugar in small jug until
smooth; gradually whisk in
oil, in a thin steady stream,
until thickened.
prep time 5 minutes
makes 1 cup
**nutritional count per
tablespoon** 12.1g total fat
(1.7g saturated fat); 456kJ
(109 cal); 0.4g carbohydrate;
0g protein; 0g fibre

Ranch dressing

½ cup (150g) mayonnaise
¼ cup (60ml) buttermilk
1 tablespoon white wine
   vinegar
1 small brown onion (80g),
   chopped finely
1 clove garlic, crushed
1 tablespoon finely chopped
   fresh chives
1 tablespoon finely chopped
   fresh flat-leaf parsley
¼ teaspoon sweet paprika

1 Whisk ingredients in small
jug until combined.
prep time 10 minutes
makes 1 cup
**nutritional count per
tablespoon** 4.2g total fat
(0.5g saturated fat); 217kJ
(52 cal); 3.2g carbohydrate;
0.5g protein; 0.2g fibre

Italian dressing

⅔ cup (160ml) olive oil
⅓ cup (80ml)
   white wine vinegar
1 clove garlic, crushed
1 teaspoon caster sugar
2 teaspoons finely chopped
   fresh oregano
2 teaspoons finely chopped
   fresh basil
1 fresh long red chilli,
   chopped finely

1 Combine ingredients in
screw-top jar; shake well.
prep time 5 minutes
makes 1 cup
**nutritional count per
tablespoon** 12.2g total fat
(1.7g saturated fat); 464kJ
(111 cal); 0.4g carbohydrate;
0.1g protein; 0.2g fibre

Silver beets

VARIETIES

1. Silver beet Although it is often confused with english spinach, silver beet is a very different vegetable; it has darker green, stiff and crinkly leaves, is sturdier than spinach and does not break down as much during cooking. It is, in fact, part of the beet family rather than the spinach family, a fact reflected in the robust texture of its leaves and wide edible stems.

2. Red silver beet has a red stem, ribs and can have either red or green leaves.

3. Rainbow silver beet can have a stem of a variety of colours: red, purple, yellow or cream. Adds great colour to salads.

Silver beet is also known as swiss chard, chard or blettes, and is sometimes labelled as such at the greengrocer. Silver beet suits the flavours of the Mediterranean menu – garlic, sultanas, tomato, pine nuts, lemon and olive oil – and it makes a great Italian soup in a clear broth with white beans. It is available all year.

CHOOSE bunches that have glossy, dark green leaves and crisp-looking stems.

STORE unwashed in the refrigerator for up to 3 days.

PREPARE the leaves for cooking by trimming them from the thick white stem, which is used separately. Wash silver beet thoroughly in cold water as the crinkly leaves hide much grit and dirt. Because the leaves of the silver beet are tough, it is a good idea to chop them finely for easier eating. Strip the stringy bits from the outer skin of the stem using a vegetable peeler, then chop the stem finely.

BLANCH whole leaves, uncovered, in a large pot of boiling water for about 2 minutes.

MICROWAVE Silver beet is suitable for cooking in the microwave oven.

STIR-FRY silver beet for about 1 minute.

PAN-FRY finely chopped leaves, especially with onion and bacon, over medium heat until the leaves have broken down. Use the mixture as a filling for lasagne, as the base flavour for a quiche, or mix with ricotta and use in place of spinach in a spinach pie.

BRAISE Place finely chopped silver beet, a little butter, salt and pepper and enough chicken or vegetable stock to cover the silver beet in a shallow flameproof dish with a tight-fitting lid. Cook, covered, in the oven at 200°C/180°C fan-forced for 20 minutes, then uncover and continue cooking until the sauce is thickened.

ADD chopped leaves and stems to a soup or stew near the end of the cooking time. The stems should cook for a little longer than the leaves, so add these first.

Silver beet, cheese and fillo stacks

4 sheets fillo pastry
40g butter, melted
1 tablespoon olive oil
1 medium brown onion (150g), chopped finely
1 clove garlic, crushed
2 rindless bacon rashers (130g), chopped finely
1kg silver beet, trimmed, shredded finely
2 tablespoons lemon juice
200g ricotta cheese
100g fetta cheese, crumbled

1 Preheat oven to 200°C/180°C fan-forced. Grease oven trays.
2 Place one sheet of pastry on board; brush with butter, top with another pastry sheet. Repeat layering with pastry and butter. Cut pastry stack in half widthways; place on tray. Grease base of another similar-sized oven tray; place on top of pastry stack (this is to stop the pastry from puffing up too much). Bake about 12 minutes or until browned. Cut each fillo stack into 9 rectangles (you will have 18 rectangles).
3 Meanwhile, heat oil in large deep saucepan; cook onion, garlic and bacon, stirring, until onion softens and bacon is crisp. Add silver beet and juice; cook, covered, stirring occasionally, until silver beet is wilted and tender. Remove from heat; stir in cheeses.
4 Place one fillo rectangle on each serving plate; top equally with half the silver beet mixture then another fillo rectangle. Top with remaining silver beet mixture and remaining fillo rectangles.
prep & cook time 30 minutes **serves** 6
nutritional count per serving 19.6g total fat (10.1g saturated fat); 1162kJ (278 cal); 8.9g carbohydrate; 14.5g protein; 5.1g fibre

Spinach

Popeye's favourite vegetable is indeed packed with iron and other nutrients. Spinach, also known as english spinach, has tender, green leaves and an earthy 'green' flavour, which can sometimes be a little tart. Baby spinach leaves (*pictured page 86*) are slightly more tender and a little less tart than the mature leaves. Baby spinach leaves are discussed further in the Salad Greens chapter (*see page 85*). Spinach goes well with bacon, onion, nutmeg, pine nuts, prosciutto or pancetta, and mild-flavoured cheeses such as ricotta or mascarpone, or salty cheeses such as fetta or parmesan. The creamed spinach recipe (*see this page*) is an undeniably good side dish to a traditional Hungarian meal of veal schnitzel, mash and pickled cucumbers. Spinach is available all year.

CHOOSE bright green, healthy-looking leaves with a crisp stem. If you can, buy spinach in a bunch as it keeps better this way. Be aware that spinach cooks down to a mere third of its uncooked quantity – so buy plenty. One average bunch makes about enough for a side dish for two people.

STORE the unwashed bunch of spinach, with the string loosened, in the refrigerator for up to 2 days.

PREPARE For an extra smooth spinach puree, remove the entire central stem from the leaf; otherwise, simply cut the stem from below the leaf. After removing the stems washing well is imperative as the leaves can harbour grit and small bugs. If you need dry spinach for your recipe, put it in a salad spinner and gently spin to remove excess water.

RAW chopped spinach leaves can be tossed into a salad, pasta, soup, stir-fry or stew just before serving. Add to gnocchi or pasta dough for a different flavour and green colour.

BLANCH leaves in boiling water for 1 minute only. Drain well after cooking by pressing into the bottom of a colander set over the sink. Chopped, blanched and drained spinach makes a beautiful filling for a pie, frittata, quiche or ravioli.

STEAM for 3 minutes, or until wilted, tossing once during cooking time.

MICROWAVE Spinach is suitable to be cooked in the microwave oven until just wilted; refresh under cold water and drain well.

STIR-FRY spinach for about 30 seconds.

PAN-FRY for 2 to 4 minutes, moving the pan constantly. Wilt washed, drained, but not dried, coarsely chopped spinach in a frying pan with butter, lemon juice and garlic to make a bed for fish or chicken fillets.

Creamed spinach

20g butter
600g spinach, trimmed
½ cup (125ml) cream

1 Melt butter in large frying pan; cook spinach, stirring, until wilted.
2 Add cream; bring to the boil. Reduce heat; simmer, uncovered, until liquid reduces by half.
prep & cook time 15 minutes **serves** 4
nutritional count per serving 38.7g total fat (25.4g saturated fat); 1555kJ (372 cal); 2.8g carbohydrate; 3.5g protein; 2.1g fibre

Swedes

A winter root vegetable, the swede, or rutabaga, is used similarly to a potato in stews, mash and hearty warming soups. They have a surprisingly fresh, nutty taste, and a slightly crisp texture, even when cooked. Swedes have a creamy white flesh that becomes golden when cooked. A sign of a very good swede, grown in the cool climate it loves, is its very orange colouring. Pair swede with other root vegetables, such as turnip or pumpkin, or with fresh-flavoured herbs like thyme and mint, or with earthy flavours like mushrooms. Or simply enjoy as a nuttier-tasting alternative to potato.

CHOOSE swedes that feel heavy for their size without any soft spots. Rough blemishes are not a sign of a bad swede; they are an imperfect-looking vegetable.

STORE in a cool, dark, dry place for up to 3 weeks once leaves have been trimmed.

PREPARE Peel swede thickly to remove both the thin outer skin and the thicker skin under it; this layer can be quite bitter after cooking if not removed properly.

BOIL Add only enough water to cover swede, then boil, covered, about 15 minutes or until tender.

STEAM for about 20 minutes or until tender.

MICROWAVE Swede is suitable to cook in a microwave oven.

Combine mashed swede with cream and herbs, or carrot or potato.

ROAST swede for 45 minutes to 1 hour at 200°C/180°C fan-forced.

BRAISE chopped swede in stock or wine in the oven until tender then finish over high heat on the stovetop.

ADD to a stew or casserole with other winter vegetables.

Chilli and herb swede crush

1kg swedes, chopped coarsely
40g butter
¼ cup (60ml) cream
1 fresh long red chilli, chopped finely
1 tablespoon finely chopped fresh flat-leaf parsley
2 teaspoons finely grated lemon rind

1 Boil, steam or microwave swede until tender; drain.
2 Coarsely crush swede with butter and cream in medium bowl. Stir in remaining ingredients.
prep & cook time 30 minutes **serves** 4
nutritional count per serving 14.7g total fat (9.7g saturated fat); 773kJ (185 cal); 8.6g carbohydrate; 2.3g protein; 5.8g fibre

Sweet potatoes

VARIETIES

1. Kumara, or orange sweet potato, is the most popular variety; its musky, sweet flavour makes it a favourite. Kumara is the Polynesian name for this vegetable.

2. Purple sweet potato has a white flesh that discolours when cut. Drop cut pieces into icy water as you go to keep this from happening.

3. White sweet potato is less sweet than the other varieties having an earthy flavour. It has purple flesh beneath the white skin and is best for baking.

Sweet potato has a sweet, nutty flavour and a soft texture that kids love, which makes it an excellent alternative to pumpkin. It also has a low GI rating, giving a long, slow release of energy. Use sweet potato as you would pumpkin or potato. It also works well in place of pumpkin in sweet or savoury pies, muffins or breads.

CHOOSE firm, heavy, sweet potatoes with a deep colour.

STORE in a cool, dark, dry place for up to a week.

PREPARE for roasting by scrubbing rather than peeling to retain as much of the nutrients present in the skin as possible. For mash, peel with a vegetable peeler then chop coarsely.

BOIL. Add just enough water to cover coarsely chopped sweet potato then boil, covered, about 15 minutes.

STEAM coarsely chopped pieces for about 15 minutes.

MICROWAVE Sweet potato is suitable to cook in a microwave oven.

Coarsely mash sweet potato with butter, salt and pepper for a delicious alternative to mashed potato.

STIR-FRY finely sliced sweet potato for 3 to 5 minutes.

DEEP-FRY thin layers of sweet potato stripped with a vegetable peeler.

GRILL or BARBECUE thin slices until tender for a smoky flavour that really suits sweet potato.

ROAST Sweet potato doesn't cook to a crunch, like potatoes, rather, it breaks down into a delicious, melting, caramelised treat. If you are having roast potatoes, too, put the sweet potatoes in slightly after the potatoes as they cook faster. Roast for 45 to 60 minutes at 200°C/180°C fan-forced.

BLEND or PUREE boiled, steamed or microwaved kumara with chicken or vegetable stock; add cumin and chilli flakes to make a delicious earthy soup.

Sweet potato crisps with chilli salt

1 medium kumara (400g)
1 medium white sweet potato (400g)
1 medium purple sweet potato (400g)
vegetable oil, for deep-frying
2 teaspoons sea salt flakes
½ teaspoon dried chilli flakes
½ teaspoon sweet paprika

1 Using vegetable peeler, slice vegetables into long, thin strips.
2 Heat oil in wok; deep-fry kumara and sweet potato strips, in batches, until browned lightly and crisp. Drain on wire rack over paper-lined tray.
3 Combine salt, chilli and paprika in small bowl. Sprinkle hot sweet potato crisps with chilli salt mixture.
prep & cook time 25 minutes **serves** 4
nutritional count per serving 13.2g total fat (1.6g saturated fat); 1254kJ (300 cal); 38.7g carbohydrate; 4.4g protein; 4.8g fibre
tip Kumara requires longer frying than other sweet potato varieties. For best results, deep-fry kumara separately first.

Tomatoes

It is lucky tomatoes are available for us to eat year round as they are almost indispensable in the kitchen. Tomatoes are packed with vitamin C and lycopene, which is believed to help prevent some cancers. A true sun-ripened tomato is one of the most delicious things you'll ever eat.

The skin of the tomato is responsible for the fresh tomato aroma, and the wall (fleshy part) of the tomato contains most of the sugars. The seeds and liquid have double the acid found in other parts of the tomato, which makes them bitter. Removing the skin and seeds of tomatoes is necessary in sòme recipes to achieve the correct balance of flavour.

Olive oil, basil, salt and pepper is one of the simplest and most common dressings for tomato – for good reason, it is delicious. Garlic, red onion, mild cheeses, oregano, rosemary, chilli, grilled meat or white fish are all fine companions for the tomato.

6.

5.

2.

3.

2.

8.

VARIETIES

1. Oxheart tomatoes are only available in late summer. It is very large and can weigh up to 250g. It is known for its exceptional taste and meaty flesh, so is glorious for eating raw although it also cooks well. It has a thick wall and a strong structure, which is good for sandwiches, salads and chopping.

2. Cherry, baby roma and grape are tiny tomatoes that burst with flavour in your mouth. They are usually very sweet when compared to normal-sized tomatoes.

3. Yellow teardrop are bright yellow baby tomatoes, and are a great colourful addition to a tomato salad. The flavour is not quite as sweet as red cherry tomatoes.

4. Kumatos are available from specialist grocers. They are a slightly sweet, black-coloured tomato – perfect for adding some colour and texture to a tomato salad.

5. Roma or plum are egg-shaped tomatoes used a lot in Italian cooking. They are the best tomatoes for drying and making tomato-based sauces. They have a relatively thick wall, which contains the sugars, so are known for being consistently sweet.

6. Round tomatoes are the garden variety supermarket tomato; they are better used in recipes where they are cooked, such as in sauces.

7. Green tomatoes are simply tomatoes that haven't ripened yet, although they are fine to eat, particularly grilled.

8. Vine-ripened tomatoes have an incredible aroma and a bright red flesh. They are often more expensive than other varieties, and are usually full of flavour.

CHOOSE tomatoes that feel firm, but not too firm. Buying them green is no problem, as they ripen easily at room temperature out of the sun, and ripen even more quickly in a brown paper bag with a banana. Blemishes are also no problem, just make sure there are no spots softer than the rest of the tomato.

STORE at room temperature for up to 4 days once very ripe. Chilling reduces the flavour and hinders the ripening process.

PREPARE For a tomato sauce, it is best to seed the tomato, but leave the skin on and strain it off later. This method retains the aromas in the skin and avoids the bitterness of the seeds. However, due to time restraints, straining is often not an option, and most people simply peel the tomatoes before cooking.

TO PEEL, cut a small cone around the core at the top of the tomato using a small sharp knife and remove it, then cut a small cross in the skin at the base of the tomato. Plunge tomatoes in boiling water for one minute then remove with tongs or a slotted spoon. Let them cool in a bowl of cold water, then slide a knife under the skin at the base and peel off. To peel uncooked tomatoes, use a vegetable peeler; this may take a little practice.

TO REMOVE SEEDS, halve the tomato, then squeeze and scrape out the seeds. If you want to separate the juice from the seeds, do this over a strainer. The strained juice can be added to the recipe, if you like, but discard the bitter seeds. Chop the tomato as required for the recipe.

RAW tomato has myriad uses; in salads and salsas, on sandwiches, mixed with a mild cheese or chopped into a mix for a pasta or bruschetta topping. Many great cooks list their favourite meal as thinly sliced ripe tomato on buttered toast, with nothing more than a few flakes of sea salt and a twist of ground black pepper.

STIR-FRY tomato for about 3 to 5 minutes.

ROAST tomatoes are great as an accompaniment to a meat dish, or used in a soup or sauce for a deeper flavour. Halve the tomatoes and sprinkle the cut side with salt and pepper. Roast at 220°C/200°C fan-forced, uncovered, for 30 minutes. Combine some onion halves and unpeeled garlic with the tomatoes to enhance the flavour.

BARBECUE or GRILL tomato halves for a smoky flavour.

STEW tomatoes to make a sauce that can be used for pasta or as the basis for many Italian recipes.

PICKLE Make a chutney or relish with chilli, onion and sultanas. Use this on sandwiches, burgers or with a strong cheddar on a cheese platter.

Make a shallow incision in the base of the tomato then plunge it into boiling water. The skin peels easily away in strips.

Halve the tomatoes and squeeze out the seeds and juice.

Basic tomato pasta sauce

2 tablespoons olive oil
1 small brown onion (80g),
    chopped finely
1 clove garlic, crushed
2kg ripe tomatoes, peeled,
    seeded, chopped coarsely
⅓ cup loosely packed fresh
    basil leaves

1 Heat oil in large saucepan; cook onion and garlic, stirring, until onion softens.
2 Add tomato and basil; cook, stirring, 5 minutes or until tomato begins to soften. Bring to the boil. Reduce heat; simmer, uncovered, stirring occasionally, 40 minutes or until sauce thickens.
3 Serve over cooked pasta.

prep & cook time 1 hour **makes** 2 cups
nutritional count per ¼ cup 4.8g total fat (0.6g saturated fat); 343kJ (82 cal); 5.4g carbohydrate; 2.7g protein; 3.3g fibre

Mixed tomato caprese salad

4 small green tomatoes (360g), sliced thinly
4 small black tomatoes (360g), sliced thinly
4 small vine-ripened tomatoes (360g), sliced thinly
4 bocconcini cheese (240g), sliced thinly
⅓ cup coarsely chopped fresh basil
2 tablespoons olive oil
1 tablespoon balsamic vinegar

1 Layer tomato, cheese and basil on serving plate; drizzle with combined oil and vinegar.

prep time 20 minutes **serves** 4
nutritional count per serving 18.5g total fat (7.3g saturated fat); 1020kJ (244 cal); 5.2g carbohydrate; 13.1g protein; 3.3g fibre

Turnips

The turnip has a sweetly bitter taste that is milder than its close relative, the swede. These winter vegetables are excellent in a stew or roasted. Baby turnips are sweeter, with a delicate flavour. Cooking for too long produces an overcooked cabbage flavour. Season turnip with Moroccan spices and pair with red meat.

CHOOSE firm, white turnips with very green leaves.

STORE turnip with its leaves lopped off (but don't discard them as they can be cooked and eaten like spinach on the day of purchase). Turnips will then keep for up to 2 weeks in the refrigerator.

PREPARE for cooking by thickly peeling the bitter skin and roughly chopping.

RAW baby turnip is crunchy and fresh-tasting; slice thinly or coarsely grate into a salad or onto a sandwich.

BRAISE chopped pieces in a little stock and cook in the oven or on the stovetop over a low heat until tender.

BOIL Add just enough water to cover coarsely chopped medium-sized turnips then boil, covered, for about 10 minutes or until tender. Test for tenderness during cooking with a knife to avoid overcooking.

STEAM medium-sized turnips for about 12 minutes or until tender.

MICROWAVE Turnips are suitable to cook in a microwave oven.

ROAST mature turnips, plain, or combined with olive oil, garlic, a sprinkling of brown sugar and some cumin seeds at about 200°C/180°C fan-forced for about 30 minutes or until browned.

MASH cooked turnip with cooked potatoes, a little cream and some parmesan cheese for a sweet, creamy turnip mash.

Moroccan turnip soup

1 tablespoon olive oil

1 large brown onion (200g), chopped coarsely

2 cloves garlic, crushed

2 teaspoons cumin seeds

2 teaspoons ground coriander

½ teaspoon hot paprika

1.5kg turnips, trimmed, chopped coarsely

1.5 litres (6 cups) chicken stock

½ cup (125ml) cream

⅓ cup coarsely chopped fresh flat-leaf parsley

1 Heat oil in large saucepan; cook onion and garlic, stirring, until onion softens. Add spices; cook, stirring, until fragrant. Add turnip and stock; bring to the boil. Reduce heat; simmer, uncovered, until turnips are tender.

2 Blend or process soup, in batches, until smooth.

3 Return soup to same pan with cream; stir until hot.

4 Serve bowls of soup sprinkled with parsley.

prep & cook time 50 minutes **serves** 4

nutritional count per serving 19.7g total fat (10.3g saturated fat); 1267kJ (303 cal); 17.5g carbohydrate; 9.9g protein; 10g fibre

Witlof

Witlof, or belgian endive (US), or chicory (UK) has a tightly bunched, elongated head. To minimise bitterness it is grown in the dark, which also keeps its leaves white with just a hint of pale yellow or burgundy at the tips. It is mildly bitter, crunchy and its lovely shaped leaves make it perfect for presenting entrée-sized morsels of salty cheese, crisp prosciutto or creamy crab salad. When cooked, its delicate bitterness is the perfect accompaniment to mild food, or as a foil to rich dishes.

CHOOSE firm, tightly bunched witlof. As witlof is exposed to light, it becomes less white and more bitter, so choose those that are as pale as possible in the white sections.

STORE unwashed witlof for up to 2 days in the refrigerator in a brown paper bag to reduce its exposure to light.

PREPARE witlof by removing any damaged outer leaves. If you are cooking witlof whole, brush it clean with a damp cloth rather than soaking it in water. If you are using the leaves separately, cut 2cm to 3cm off the base then pull the leaves away. As the leaves get closer to the centre, you will find them more difficult to remove, so cut a little more from the base then continue removing the leaves. To clean, wipe each individual leaf. Witlof 'rusts' where it is cut with a knife so do so at the last possible moment.

RAW witlof is an excellent salad green, and a delicious edible vessel for creamy salad entrées.

STIR-FRY wiflof for about 1 minute.

BRAISE One of the best ways to cook witlof is to braise it in stock. Rub witlof with a little butter, sprinkle with salt and pepper and place in a shallow flameproof dish with a tight-fitting lid and enough chicken or vegetable stock to reach halfway up the witlof. Cook, covered, in the oven at 200°C/180°C fan-forced for 20 minutes, then uncover and continue cooking until witlof is tender and the sauce reduced and thickened.

GRILL or BARBECUE halved witlof until wilted to bring out the sweetness in the leaves. This makes a very attractive side dish to barbecued or grilled meat and fish.

Witlof, pear and blue cheese salad

2 red witlof (250g), trimmed, leaves separated
2 yellow witlof (250g), trimmed, leaves separated
1 medium pear (230g), sliced thinly
¾ cup (90g) roasted pecans, coarsely chopped
blue cheese dressing
⅓ cup (80ml) buttermilk
100g blue cheese, crumbled
1 tablespoon lemon juice

1 Make blue cheese dressing.
2 Combine salad ingredients in large bowl.
3 Serve salad drizzled with blue cheese dressing.
blue cheese dressing Whisk ingredients in small jug until smooth.
prep time 20 minutes **serves** 4
nutritional count per serving 24.9g total fat (6.5g saturated fat); 1295kJ (309 cal); 9.9g carbohydrate; 9.5g protein; 5.3g fibre

2.

1.

1.

3.

3.

4.

3.

Zucchini & squash

VARIETIES

1. Green and yellow zucchini taste the same. Use a combination of colours for effect. Zucchini grow very quickly from the flowering stage to the zucchini stage, and the smaller they are, the sweeter they will be. Zucchini has a generally mild, slightly acidic and sweet flavour with a spongy flesh that softens when cooked.

2. Lebanese, or grey or white zucchini are sometimes considered to have a superior taste to the green and yellow varieties. They are thicker and smaller in size. They can be prepared and eaten in the same way as other zucchini.

3. Squash, pattypan, or button squash range in colour from pale green to yellow and have a sweet flavour that is very similar to zucchini. Take care not to cook squash too little or too much, as the taste and texture can suffer greatly from either.

4. Zucchini flowers are a delicacy gaining in popularity. The flowers have a subtle zucchini flavour. They are usually stuffed with a mild-flavoured filling and either served as is or deep fried in a light batter. They are limited in supply by their delicate structure and short growing season as they rapidly develop into the zucchini gourd. They are available in summer.

Mediterranean dishes are often lost without zucchini; they make up an essential ingredient in ratatouille, and pair well with tomatoes, onion, butter, olive oil, garlic, chilli, lemon and herbs such as dill, sage and thyme. They also appear regularly in Indian dishes. Zucchini cooked with cumin, yogurt or cooked in a curry is delicious.

CHOOSE unblemished, firm, glossy zucchini and squash.

STORE zucchini and squash for up to 4 days in a plastic bag in the refrigerator. Eat zucchini flowers on the day you buy them.

PREPARE Zucchini do not require peeling, although strips peeled in intervals can increase the tenderness of a large zucchini. Simply top and tail both zucchini and squash before proceeding with your recipe.

RAW grated zucchini or squash can be tossed through warm pasta, or into a salad.

BOIL Avoid boiling zucchini and squash as they become waterlogged and insipid when cooked this way.

STEAM zucchini and squash for 6 minutes or until tender.

MICROWAVE Zucchini and squash are suitable to cook in a microwave oven.

STIR-FRY finely chopped zucchini or squash for 2 to 4 minutes.

PAN-FRY Peel zucchini into fine ribbons using a vegetable peeler; pan-fry in butter, garlic and herbs about 2 minutes or until soft then toss through warm pasta. Stir coarsely grated zucchini and squash into a fritter batter and pan-fry for a breakfast treat.

DEEP-FRY stuffed zucchini flowers in a light batter until crisp.

GRILL or BARBECUE thin slices until tender for a smoky flavour, then marinate in olive oil and use in an antipasto platter, on a burger or toss through pasta for a last-minute meal.

BRAISE in a little water and butter in a frying pan for 3 to 5 minutes.

STUFF To stuff zucchini flowers, remove the stamen from inside the flower, then pipe or push the stuffing into the cavity. Twist the top of the flower petals together to seal.

Open out the petals of the flower and pinch out the stamen inside.

Use a piping bag to fill the cavity with stuffing. Twist tips of petals together to close.

Lemon and ricotta-filled zucchini flowers

250g ricotta cheese

2 tablespoons finely grated parmesan cheese

1 teaspoon finely grated lemon rind

1 tablespoon lemon juice

1 tablespoon finely chopped fresh mint

2 tablespoons roasted pine nuts

12 zucchini flowers with stem attached (240g)

1 Combine cheeses, rind, juice, mint and nuts in small bowl.

2 Discard stamens from inside zucchini flowers; fill flowers with cheese mixture, twist petal tops to enclose filling.

3 Place zucchini flowers, in single layer, in large bamboo steamer, over large saucepan of boiling water. Steam, covered, about 20 minutes or until zucchini are tender.

prep & cook time 45 minutes **serves** 4

nutritional count per serving 13.4g total fat (5.5g saturated fat); 711kJ (170 cal); 2.2g carbohydrate; 9.6g protein; 1.4g fibre

Summer squash salad

500g yellow patty-pan squash, halved
500g green patty-pan squash, halved
200g baby new potatoes, halved
⅓ cup (80ml) olive oil
2 tablespoons lemon juice
1 clove garlic, crushed
1 tablespoon finely chopped fresh dill
250g cherry tomatoes, halved
1 cup loosely packed fresh flat-leaf parsley leaves

1 Boil, steam or microwave squash and potatoes, separately, until tender; drain.
2 Combine warm squash and potatoes with remaining ingredients in large bowl.
prep time 30 minutes **serves** 4
nutritional count per serving 18.9g total fat (2.6g saturated fat); 1191kJ (285 cal); 16.6g carbohydrate; 8.4g protein; 8.6g fibre

Equipment

Kitchen utensils that do more than just clutter up your cupboard.

1. ASPARAGUS STEAMER
Though not necessary to steam asparagus, they do it perfectly, cooking the spears upright, with the thicker, woodier bottoms in boiling water and the steam gently rising to cook the tender tips.

2. VEGETABLE PEELERS
These come in a variety of shapes. They all do a good job and at least one is necessary in the kitchen. Choose your vegetable peeler based on how comfortable it is to hold.

3. V-SLICER OR MANDOLIN
This gadget allows you to cut vegetables into wafer-thin slices. There are several attachments allowing you to choose how thick or thin you want your slices. Some models also have a julienne setting. The blades are extremely sharp, so store carefully.

4. TOMATO CORER This scoop easily removes the core of the tomato, so there is no need for fiddly cutting with a sharp pointed knife.

1.

3.

2.

2.

2.

2.

4.

5. SALAD SPINNER Drying washed leaves in a tea towel can be laborious and mostly ineffective. The spinner uses a centrifugal force to gently remove water from the leaves.

6. COLANDER This is an indispensable tool for draining liquid from solids. Comes with wide holes and a base so it can stand on its own. It can be made of plastic, metal or ceramic.

7. AVOCADO SLICER Scoop the flesh out of a deseeded avocado with the round edge scraping the inside of the skin. The wires cut the flesh into wedges.

8. PLASTIC LETTUCE KNIFE Many leafy vegetables 'rust' (oxidise) when cut with a metal knife. This hard plastic knife has a serrated edge, so the cut edge will no longer 'rust'. Can be used safely on non-stick bakeware, too.

9. CAN OPENER There are two main varieties; one removes the lid from the inside of the lip and the other removes the lid and the lip. The former is a safer option, as there is no sharp edge left on the can, but the lid easily drops into the can once cut. The latter leaves a sharp edge on the top of the can.

10. JULIENNE PEELER These are designed to peel vegetables into long thin strips. They have very sharp teeth, so take care when using this utensil.

11. BEAN STRINGER This kitchen tool removes the ends and the strings from green beans and thinly slices them lengthways.

12. CORN STRIPPER Gripping the husked corn cob in one hand and the stripper in the other, scrape in a downwards motion with the little serrated edge positioned behind the kernels and against the cob. Move in strips around the cob until all kernals are removed.

5.

6.

10.

7.

8.

9.

11.

12.

Glossary

ACIDULATED WATER water to which lemon juice has been added to prevent cut surfaces of foods from discolouring.

ARBORIO RICE small round-grain rice well suited to absorb a large amount of liquid; especially good in risottos.

BACON RASHERS also known as bacon slices.

BASIL an aromatic herb; there are many types, but the most commonly used is sweet, or common, basil.

BREAD

ciabatta in Italian, the word means "slipper", the shape of this popular white bread with a crisp crust.

french stick a long, narrow cylindrical loaf with a crisp brown crust and a light chewy interior. Also known as french loaf or french bread.

pitta also known as lebanese bread. A wheat-flour pocket bread sold in large, flat pieces that separate into two thin rounds. Also available in small pieces called pocket pitta.

BREADCRUMBS, PACKAGED fine, crunchy, purchased breadcrumbs.

BUTTER use salted or unsalted (sweet) butter; 125g is equal to one stick (4 ounces) of butter.

BUTTERMILK originally the term given to the slightly sour liquid left after butter was churned from cream, today it is made similarly to yogurt. Sold alongside all fresh milk products in supermarkets. Despite its name, it is low in fat.

CAPERS the grey-green buds of a warm climate (usually Mediterranean) shrub, sold either dried and salted, or pickled in a vinegar brine. Baby capers are picked early, and are smaller, fuller-flavoured and more expensive than the full-sized ones. Rinse well before using.

CARAWAY available in seed or ground form. Adds a sharp anise flavour to dishes.

CHEESE

blue mould-treated cheese mottled with blue veining. Includes firm and crumbly stilton types to mild, creamy brie-like cheeses.

bocconcini a walnut-sized baby mozzarella. A delicate, semi-soft, white cheese; spoils rapidly, so keep refrigerated, in brine, for two days at most.

fetta Greek in origin; a crumbly goat- or sheep-milk cheese with a sharp salty taste.

mozzarella a soft, spun-curd cheese. Has a low melting point and elastic texture; is used to add texture rather than flavour.

parmesan also known as parmigiana; a hard, grainy cows-milk cheese.

ricotta a sweet, moist, soft, white, cows-milk cheese; has a slightly grainy texture.

CHILLI available in many types and sizes. Use rubber gloves when seeding and chopping fresh chillies as they can burn your skin. Remove seeds and membranes to lessen the heat.

flakes crushed dried chillies.

long red available fresh and dried; a generic term used for any moderately hot, long, thin chilli (about 6cm to 8cm long).

thai red also known as "scuds"; small and very hot.

CINNAMON dried inner bark of the shoots of the cinnamon tree; comes in stick (quill) or ground form.

CORIANDER also known as pak chee, cilantro or chinese parsley; bright-green leafy herb with a pungent flavour. Coriander seeds are also available but are no substitute for fresh coriander, as the taste is very different.

CORNMEAL often called polenta, to which this ground corn (maize) is similar, albeit coarser. One can be substituted for the other, but textures will vary.

CREAM we used fresh cream, unless otherwise stated. Also known as pure cream and pouring cream.

sour cream thick, commercially-cultured soured cream.

CUMIN also known as zeera or comino; has a spicy, nutty flavour. Available in seed, dried and ground forms.

DISGORGE to draw out bitter juices from a vegetable by sprinkling cut surfaces with salt.

DILL also known as dill weed; used fresh or dried. It has a sweet anise/celery flavour.

EGG some recipes in this book may call for raw or barely cooked eggs; exercise caution if there is a salmonella problem in your area.

FLAT-LEAF PARSLEY also known as italian or continental parsley.

FLOUR

plain an all-purpose flour made from wheat.

self-raising plain flour combined with baking powder in the proportion of 1 cup flour to 2 teaspoons baking powder.

GINGER, FRESH also known as green or root ginger; the thick root of a tropical plant.

KAFFIR LIME LEAF is also known as bai magrood; looks like two glossy dark green leaves joined end to end to form a rounded hourglass shape. A strip of fresh lime peel may be substituted for each kaffir lime leaf.

KECAP MANIS *see sauces.*

LEMON GRASS a tall, clumping, lemon-smelling and -tasting, sharp-edged grass; the white lower part of the stem is used, chopped, in Asian cooking.

MAPLE SYRUP a thin syrup distilled from the sap of the maple tree. Maple-flavoured syrup or pancake syrup is not an adequate substitute for the real thing.

MAYONNAISE we use whole-egg mayonnaise in our recipes unless otherwise indicated.

MINT the most commonly used variety of mint is spearmint; it has pointed, bright-green leaves and a fresh flavour.

MUSTARD

dijon also known as french. A pale brown, creamy, distinctively flavoured, fairly mild mustard.

wholegrain also known as seeded; made from crushed seeds and dijon-style mustard.

NOODLES, FRESH RICE also known as ho fun, khao pun, sen yau, pho or kway tiau. Available in strands of various widths or large sheets weighing about 500g, which are cut into the noodle size desired. Chewy and pure white, they do not need pre-cooking before use.

NUTMEG the dried nut of a tree native to Indonesia; available ground or you can grate your own with a fine grater.

NUTS

almond a flat, pointy-ended nut with a pitted brown shell enclosing a creamy white kernel that is covered by a brown skin. Flaked almonds are paper-thin slices.

cashew a kidney-shaped nut with a sweet, buttery flavour. Has a high oil content so should be stored in the refrigerator.

hazelnut also known as filberts; rich, sweet, grape-sized nut having a brown inedible skin that is removed by rubbing heated nuts together vigorously in a tea towel.

macadamia a rich, buttery nut. Has a high oil content so store in the refrigerator.

pecan a golden-brown, rich, buttery nut. Walnuts can be substituted.

pine nut also known as pignoli; not in fact a nut but a small, cream-coloured kernel from pine cones.

walnut a golden-brown, rich, buttery nut formed in two distinct halves. Pecan nuts can be substituted.

OIL

macadamia pressed from ground macadamia nuts. Available in some supermarkets and delicatessens.

olive made from ripened olives. Extra virgin and virgin are the first and second press of the olive and are considered the best, while extra light or light refers to taste, not fat levels.

peanut pressed from ground peanuts; the most commonly used oil in Asian cooking because of its high smoke point (capacity to handle high heat without burning).

sesame made from roasted, crushed white sesame seeds; more often used as a flavouring rather than a cooking medium.

vegetable sourced from plants.

ORECCHIETTE PASTA small disc-shaped pasta; translates literally as "little ears".

OREGANO a herb, also known as wild marjoram; has a woody stalk and clumps of tiny, dark-green leaves. Has a pungent, peppery flavour.

PANCETTA an Italian unsmoked bacon; pork belly is cured in salt and spices then rolled into a sausage shape and dried for several weeks.

PAPRIKA ground dried, sweet red capsicum (bell pepper); there are many types available, including sweet, hot, mild and smoked.

PASTRY, READY-ROLLED packaged sheets of frozen pastry, available from supermarkets.

fillo is unique in that no fat or margarine is added to the dough. The dough is very elastic in texture and not rolled like other pastries, but stretched to the desired thickness. This gives it its delicate, tissue-thin sheets. It is best brushed with butter or margarine before baking.

puff a crisp, light pastry; layers of dough and margarine are folded and rolled many times making many layers. When baked, it becomes a high, crisp, flaky pastry.

PEPPERCORNS, BLACK the berry is picked when not quite ripe, then dried until it shrivels and the skin turns dark brown to black.

PROSCIUTTO a kind of Italian ham; air-cured (unsmoked), salted and aged, it is usually eaten uncooked.

ROSEMARY pungent herb with long, thin pointy leaves; available fresh or dried.

SALMON FILLETS has few bones and a red-pink firm flesh with a moist, delicate flavour.

SAUCES

barbecue a spicy, tomato-based sauce used to marinate or baste, or as a condiment.

fish also called nam pla or nuoc nam; made from pulverised salted fermented fish, most often anchovies. Has a pungent smell and a strong taste, so use sparingly.

kecap manis a dark, thick sweet soy sauce; the sweetness comes from the addition of either molasses or palm sugar when brewed.

oyster Asian in origin, this rich, brown sauce is made from oysters and their brine, cooked with salt and soy sauce, and thickened with starches.

soy made from fermented soya beans. Several variations are available in most supermarkets and Asian food stores. We use japanese soy sauce, unless otherwise indicated.

Dark soy is deep brown, almost black in colour; rich, with a thicker consistency than other types. Has a pungent taste, but is not particularly salty.

Japanese soy is an all-purpose low-sodium soy sauce made with more wheat content than its Chinese counterparts. Possibly the best table soy and the one to choose if you only want one variety.

Light soy is fairly thin and, while paler than the others, is the saltiest tasting; used in dishes in which the natural colour of the ingredients is to be maintained. Not to be confused with salt-reduced or low-sodium soy sauces.

sweet chilli a mild sauce made from red thai chillies, sugar, garlic and vinegar.

Tabasco brand name of an extremely fiery sauce made from vinegar, red thai chillies and salt.

tomato pasta a prepared sauce made of a blend of tomatoes, herbs and spices.

vegetarian mushroom oyster a "vegetarian" oyster sauce made from blended mushrooms and soy sauce.

worcestershire a dark coloured condiment made from garlic, soy sauce, tamarind, onions, molasses, lime, anchovies, vinegar and seasonings.

XO a spicy seafood sauce made of scallops, dried fish and shrimp and cooked with chilli, onion, garlic and oil.

SPAGHETTI long, thin solid strands of pasta.

STOCK available in cans, tetra packs or bottles. Stock cubes or powder can also be used. As a guide, 1 teaspoon of stock powder or 1 small crumbled stock cube plus 1 cup water will give a fairly strong stock.

SUGAR

brown an extremely soft, finely granulated sugar retaining molasses for its characteristic colour and flavour.

caster also known as superfine or finely granulated table sugar.

white a coarse, granulated table sugar, also known as crystal sugar.

TAHINI a rich, sesame-seed paste, used in most Middle-Eastern cuisines, especially Lebanese, in dips and sauces.

TARRAGON an aromatic herb with an anise-like flavour; available fresh, dried and powdered. Store in a plastic bag in the fridge with a damp paper towel, or stems down in a glass of water with a plastic bag on top.

THYME a member of the mint family; it has tiny grey-green leaves that give off a pungent minty, light-lemon aroma. Dried thyme comes in both leaf and powdered form and should be stored in a cool, dark place for no more than three months. Fresh thyme should be stored in the refrigerator, wrapped in a damp paper towel and placed in a sealed bag for no more than a few days.

TOFU also known as bean curd; made from the "milk" of crushed soya beans. Comes fresh as soft or firm, and processed as fried or pressed dried sheets. Leftover fresh tofu can be refrigerated in water, which is changed daily, for up to four days.

VINEGAR

balsamic made from the juice of Trebbiano grapes; it is a deep, rich brown colour with a sweet and sour flavour. There are many balsamic vinegars on the market ranging in pungency and quality depending on how long they have been aged. Quality can be determined up to a point by price; use the most expensive sparingly.

brown malt made from fermented malt flavoured with beech shavings.

cider (apple) made from the juice of fermented apples.

red wine based on fermented red wine.

rice a clear vinegar made from fermented rice and flavoured with sugar and salt. Also known as seasoned rice vinegar.

white made from spirit of cane sugar.

white wine made from white wine.

YEAST, DRIED a raising agent used in dough making. Dried (8g sachets/2 teaspoons) and fresh compressed yeast (20g) can usually be substituted one for the other when yeast is called for in a recipe.

YOGURT we used plain yogurt unless otherwise specified.

Conversion chart

MEASURES

One Australian metric measuring cup holds approximately 250ml; one Australian metric tablespoon holds 20ml; one Australian metric teaspoon holds 5ml.

The difference between one country's measuring cups and another's is within a two- or three-teaspoon variance, and will not affect your cooking results. North America, New Zealand and the United Kingdom use a 15ml tablespoon.

All cup and spoon measurements are level. The most accurate way of measuring dry ingredients is to weigh them. When measuring liquids, use a clear glass or plastic jug with the metric markings.

We use large eggs with an average weight of 60g.

DRY MEASURES

METRIC	IMPERIAL
15g	½oz
30g	1oz
60g	2oz
90g	3oz
125g	4oz (¼lb)
155g	5oz
185g	6oz
220g	7oz
250g	8oz (½lb)
280g	9oz
315g	10oz
345g	11oz
375g	12oz (¾lb)
410g	13oz
440g	14oz
470g	15oz
500g	16oz (1lb)
750g	24oz (1½lb)
1kg	32oz (2lb)

LIQUID MEASURES

METRIC	IMPERIAL
30ml	1 fluid oz
60ml	2 fluid oz
100ml	3 fluid oz
125ml	4 fluid oz
150ml	5 fluid oz (¼ pint/1 gill)
190ml	6 fluid oz
250ml	8 fluid oz
300ml	10 fluid oz (½ pint)
500ml	16 fluid oz
600ml	20 fluid oz (1 pint)
1000ml (1 litre)	1¾ pints

LENGTH MEASURES

METRIC	IMPERIAL
3mm	⅛in
6mm	¼in
1cm	½in
2cm	¾in
2.5cm	1in
5cm	2in
6cm	2½in
8cm	3in
10cm	4in
13cm	5in
15cm	6in
18cm	7in
20cm	8in
23cm	9in
25cm	10in
28cm	11in
30cm	12in (1ft)

OVEN TEMPERATURES

These oven temperatures are only a guide for conventional ovens.
For fan-forced ovens, check the manufacturer's manual.

	°C (CELSIUS)	°F (FAHRENHEIT)	GAS MARK
Very slow	120	250	½
Slow	150	275-300	1-2
Moderately slow	160	325	3
Moderate	180	350-375	4-5
Moderately hot	200	400	6
Hot	220	425-450	7-8
Very hot	240	475	9

Index

If you like this cookbook, you'll love these...

These are just a small selection of titles available in *The Australian Women's Weekly* range on sale at selected newsagents, supermarkets or online at www.acpbooks.com.au

also available in bookstores...

TEST KITCHEN
Food director Pamela Clark
Associate food editor Alexandra Somerville
Home economist Rebecca Squadrito
Nutritional information Belinda Farlow

ACP BOOKS
General manager Christine Whiston
Editorial director Susan Tomnay
Creative director & designer Hieu Chi Nguyen
Senior editor Wendy Bryant
Director of sales Brian Cearnes
Marketing manager Bridget Cody
Business analyst Rebecca Varela
Operations manager David Scotto
Production manager Victoria Jefferys
International rights enquires Laura Bamford
lbamford@acpuk.com

ACP Books are published by ACP Magazines
a division of PBL Media Pty Limited
Group publisher, Women's lifestyle
Pat Ingram
Director of sales, Women's lifestyle
Lynette Phillips
Commercial manager, Women's lifestyle
Seymour Cohen
Marketing director, Women's lifestyle
Matthew Dominello
Public relations manager, Women's lifestyle
Hannah Deveraux
Creative director, Events, Women's lifestyle
Luke Bonnano
Research Director, Women's lifestyle
Justin Stone
ACP Magazines, Chief Executive officer
Scott Lorson
PBL Media, Chief Executive officer
Ian Law

Produced by ACP Books, Sydney.
Published by ACP Books, a division of
ACP Magazines Ltd, 54 Park St, Sydney;
GPO Box 4088, Sydney, NSW 2001.
phone (02) 9282 8618 fax (02) 9267 9438.
acpbooks@acpmagazines.com.au
www.acpbooks.com.au
Printed by Dai Nippon in Korea.

Australia Distributed by Network Services,
phone +61 2 9282 8777 fax +61 2 9264 3278
networkweb@networkservicescompany.com.au
United Kingdom Distributed by Australian
Consolidated Press (UK),
phone (01604) 642 200 fax (01604) 642 300
books@acpuk.com
New Zealand Distributed by Netlink
Distribution Company,
phone (9) 366 9966 ask@ndc.co.nz
South Africa Distributed by PSD Promotions,
phone (27 11) 392 6065/6/7
fax (27 11) 392 6079/80
orders@psdprom.co.za
Canada Distributed by Publishers Group Canada
phone (800) 663 5714 fax (800) 565 3770
service@raincoast.com

Title: Vegie stars / food director, Pamela Clark.
Publisher: Sydney : ACP Books, 2008.
ISBN: 978 186396 790 7 (pbk.)
Notes: Includes index.
Subjects: Vegetable cookery.
Other Authors/Contributors: Clark, Pamela
Also Titled: Australian women's weekly
Dewey Number: 641.5636
© ACP Magazines Ltd 2008
ABN 18 053 273 546
This publication is copyright. No part of it may be reproduced or transmitted in any form without the written permission of the publishers.

Scanpan cookware is used in the AWW Test Kitchen.
To order books, phone 136 116 (within Australia).
Send recipe enquiries to:
askpamela@acpmagazines.com.au